TURNAROUND
STRATEGIES FOR THE
SMALL CHURCH

EFFECTIVE CHURCH SERIES

RON CRANDALL
Edited by HERB MILLER

TURNAROUND STRATEGIES FOR THE SMALL CHURCH

ABINGDON PRESS
Nashville

TURNAROUND STRATEGIES FOR THE SMALL CHURCH

Library of Congress Cataloging-in-Publication Data

Crandall, Ronald K.
    Turnaround strategies for the small church/Ron Crandall: edited by Herb Miller.
        p. cm.—(Effective church series)
    Includes bibliographical references and index.
    ISBN 0-687-00467-5 (pbk.: alk. paper)
    1. Small churches.   I. Miller, Herb. II. Title. III. Series.
BV637.8.c73 1995
254—dc20
                                               94-38114
                                                 CIP

95 96 97 98 99 00 01 02 03 04 — 10 9 8 7 6 5 4 3

MANUFACTURED IN THE UNITED STATES OF AMERICA

CONTENTS

FOREWORD

"Are you going to watch that TV special this weekend?" the doctor asked her friend as they sipped coffee in the hospital doctor's lounge.

"No," the other doctor replied. "I'll be out of town."

"Too bad," she added. "But you could tape it on your VCR."

"Good idea," he said. To himself he added, "I wish I could figure out how to program it."

Among America's approximately 375,000 congregations, small-membership churches are the most prevalent species. Roughly two-thirds of all congregations average one hundred or fewer Sunday morning worshipers. Like VCRs, however, prevalence does not always equal understanding. Knowing how to program these simple-looking (but exceedingly complex) organisms remains a mystery to many of their operators. As one regional church executive said, "Amazingly little of the information on this subject has penetrated to the local level."

Crandall addresses this situation in a thorough way. His insights and practical ideas, derived from broad-based research in "turnaround" small churches, speak to every denominational family. The blending of numerous concrete examples with over-arching principles adds a depth seldom seen in small church literature.

Quoting Nat Hentoff, Bill Moyers said, "Reporting is the highest form of journalism."[1] That is especially true if the reporting is thorough and clear, and if it informs people with inspiring, how-to-do-it, transferable concepts. Crandall's reporting is excellent journalism. Like the best of preaching, it moves people forward without putting them down.

Herb Miller
Lubbock, Texas

PREFACE

To be vital or to have vitality means simply to manifest life and have energy, or to be lively. Herb Miller defines a vital congregation as one that "carries out the ministry of Jesus Christ by saying and doing what Jesus said and did."[1] In other words, vital congregations have in them and manifest to the world the life of Jesus Christ.

Turnaround Strategies for the Small Church is about revitalizing smaller churches. To revitalize means to restore to a former vitality, or bring to new life. Such language reveals several assumptions. First, it is assumed that churches described as needing a turnaround were once strong and full of life—otherwise they could not be revitalized. Second, these churches are not now experiencing and manifesting to the world the life of Jesus Christ. They may or may not know the degree to which they are sick or how close they may be to death, but survival has probably become a topic of conversation more than once. They realize they aren't what they used to be. They have lost their sense of direction.

A third assumption is that smaller churches are different in some ways from medium or larger churches, and therefore deserve special study and their own prescriptions for renewed health. This is, of course, an assumption ignored by many writers in the past and even by some today. But most research over the last twenty-five years clearly establishes that this assumption is well founded and extremely important.

Fourth, it is assumed that small churches that have declined in vitality over the years can be turned around. It is this assumption that gives thousands of faithful members and pastors of small churches hope during dark days of decay and decline. "It has happened before, it can happen again, it can happen to us."

A fifth assumption is that the real experts on small church revitalization are the persons who have experienced it firsthand—the pastors and members of revitalized small churches. Acting on that assumption, letters were sent to key judicatory leaders in over fifty denominations, asking for nominations. The actual request read as follows:

> Would you identify for us two or three of your smaller churches (under 200 members and/or 100 at worship) which have shown a remarkable turnaround in the last two to five years, including: A new sense of hope and empowerment, a new vision for mission, a new readiness to reach out to the community, a new effectiveness in evangelism, and new growth in membership/church school/worship attendance?
>
> We are especially interested in looking at churches where the community context has not changed or at least cannot account for the experienced renewal and church growth.

Over two hundred churches and pastors representing eleven denominations were recommended. Of these, 186 pastors could be contacted by letter and were asked to participate in the project by filling out a survey questionnaire. One hundred and thirty-six agreed to participate and 97 returned usable surveys. Three additional pastors were selected by the author to produce an even one hundred stories of renewal in small churches. It is this database that informs *Turnaround Strategies for the Small Church.*

A list of the pastors and churches participating in the study can be found in Appendix B. Persons interested in the full report of all findings and a detailed description of the research project are encouraged to write to the author at Asbury Theological Seminary, Wilmore, KY 40503. In the chapters that follow key findings will be reported both as practical principles and as actual experiences reported by these faithful disciples, the "experts" in revitalizing small churches.

Why do we need to talk about revitalizing or turning around smaller churches? Are all small churches in such desperate need? Of course not, no more than all large churches are vital. Nevertheless, many small churches are struggling, and every year thousands of small churches that were once vital congregations close their doors for the last time. Most of these congregations have been holding on, surviving, for years. But survival is not vitality.

Almost every church that survives its first decade or two of existence has experienced vitality. Churches are normally started with that goal in mind. A generation ago the general rule of thumb for sustained church growth was that after twenty-five to thirty years a church would plateau and begin to decline unless intentional new efforts were made to grow. However, as we approach the end of this century, church growth consultant Lyle Schaller reports that 65 to 85 percent of all churches over ten years old are shrinking in membership or plateaued.[2]

As churches look backward to a former day of strength and vitality they begin to lose their sense of confidence in what God can do in them and through them in the present day and in the future. Overwhelmingly, smaller churches over thirty years old suffer from this malady. Many members of these churches and the pastors who serve them sometimes find it nearly impossible to "rejoice in the Lord always." But the testimonies of renewal reflected in the pages that follow are powerful messages of hope. Turnaround is happening.

> Do not remember the former things,
>   or consider the things of old.
> I am about to do a new thing;
>   now it springs forth, do you not perceive it?
> . . . for I give water in the wilderness,
>   rivers in the desert,
> to give drink to my chosen people,
>   the people whom I formed for myself
> so that they might declare my praise.
> (Isa. 43:18-21)

ACKNOWLEDGMENTS

Often it is said, "The small church is like a family." And often in families and in small churches people help one another with never a thought of needing a thank-you. But saying "thank you" is important, and hearing it is important too. That is why I have looked forward to writing these few words of appreciation to some of my "family" who have made this book possible.

First, I want to express my appreciation to Herb Miller for challenging me to write the book and patiently working with me throughout the entire process.

Second, I am deeply indebted to the hundreds of small church pastors and lay persons who have generously given their time and shared their hearts, minds, and souls with me over the years and especially in this project. Without them the vision of "turnaround" I have attempted to capture in these pages would not have been possible.

Third, I am grateful to Julie Broderson and Pat Richmond without whom the all important research surveys could not have been processed or the massive amount of paperwork completed.

And finally, I want to express my love and appreciation to my wife Bonnie and to my sons Matthew and Joshua who have endured me at my worst and inspired me to be my best. This is the gift healthy families always provide for one another, and it is the gift I hope some who read these pages will find for their churches as well as for their own souls.

I

PATHWAYS TO TURNAROUND

Turnaround: "A change of allegiance, opinion, mood, or policy."

Webster

Small churches all over this nation have endured a long and difficult history of misunderstanding and neglect. The needs of these small churches and the solutions that will lead toward revitalization are both complex and difficult. And yet, I am generally optimistic.[1]

Some of us are old enough to remember windup toys. One of my favorites was a tin Jeep, which performed amazing feats. If wound and turned on by the flip of a small lever, it would whir and ding, spin around, lunge forward until it encountered some obstacle or precipice, automatically reverse itself, turn in a new direction, and move ahead once more. I found it wonderfully entertaining and worked hard to make the obstacles ever more challenging. Eventually I succeeded in stalling the vehicle by boxing it in with just the right combination of restraints. Occasionally, at least in the mind of a small boy, it even seemed to get frustrated, as it banged and bumped its way into a corner. Although it was designed with a built-in "turnaround mechanism," when it was cornered and immobilized, its energy source failed rapidly. The turning wheels slowed. The whirs and dings ceased. And as abruptly as it lunged forward with the flip of a switch, it stopped, dead.

It would be stretching things to say that I looked at all this with any deep or morbid thoughts of life and death. After all, the run-down toy required only the hands of a small boy to free it and rewind it so it could start its wonderful dance all over again. But the image of that childhood toy, cornered and out of power, comes to mind as we begin to explore strategies that enable struggling small churches to experience a turnaround.

Although most human problems require much more than a small boy's hands and the turn of a key, along the way persons emerge who seem to know how to bring renewal to human lives and endeavors. The one hundred pastors we found who successfully employed turnaround strategies in their small churches are such persons. Their formulas are not identical, but they have learned, one way or another, many of the same lessons. Each of them may not be able to describe exactly what happens in turnaround, but—whether knowing it or not—each utilizes many of the same principles discovered as necessary for turnaround to occur.

Of course, since the church is not merely a human endeavor, but the creation of God empowered by the Holy Spirit, few persons who have been involved in a genuine experience of turnaround in a local church would say the result is something they accomplished. Almost always the work of the Spirit who brings new life to old and troubled churches is connected to the lives of men and women of faith who lead God's people to a new vision, a new hope, and a new identity.

Turnaround Theories

Because the experience of decline and immobility is not unique to smaller churches in our day, concerned persons of faith have always tried to warn against the dangers and offer hope to the distraught and defeated. It could be said that the primary function of the prophets was to call God's people to "re-turn" to their identity and their covenant as the children of God. God warned the Israelites through Moses "take care that you do not forget the LORD, who

14

brought you out of the land of Egypt, out of the house of slavery. . . . remember what the LORD your God did" (Deut. 6:12; 7:18). Paul instructs the early church to "be transformed by the renewing of your minds" (Rom. 12:2). He also offers a word of hope to some of us old enough to remember windup toys: "Even though our outer nature is wasting away, our inner nature is being renewed day by day" (2 Cor. 4:16). Notice the enhanced sense of power these words have when they are hyphenated: re-member, re-turn, re-new. They remind us that God is able to do again whatever God has done before, if we will cooperate with heart, soul, mind, and strength.

The Reverend John Wesley observed in the early days of the eighteenth-century English revival that great movements of reform and revitalization seldom last long. He noted that the spiritual fires of the Protestant Reformation had grown cold even within the lifetime of Martin Luther. He feared the same for the new movement of the Spirit that he was leading. Near the end of his life he wrote:

> I am not afraid that the people called Methodists should ever cease to exist either in Europe or America. But I am afraid, lest they should only exist as a dead sect, having the form of religion without the power. And this undoubtedly will be the case, unless they hold fast both the doctrine, Spirit, and discipline with which they first set out.[2]

The reality of decline and the necessity of re-turning to God is as old as the human story.

And interest in producing turnaround is not limited to those who think in spiritual terms. We might say that the natural tendency of every activity and organization is to run down. Therefore, businesses, universities, community organizations, urban centers, and even individual persons need new beginnings or they expire. Thus, researchers in many fields such as economics, history, sociology, anthropology, and organizational development, as well as pastors, evangelists, bishops, and teachers have longed to know the secrets of turnaround. Although it would not be possible to explore all the models and theories of turnaround generated by researchers in these fields, one or two examples might reveal enough to show that similar dynamics are at work whenever new life grows in the face of death. Such a discovery should not surprise Christians who believe in "God the Father Almighty, Maker of heaven and earth."

From Organizational Development

In the 1980s one of the best selling nonfiction books was *In Search of Excellence: Lessons from America's Best-Run Companies* by T. J. Peters and R. H. Waterman. They observed the managing practices of forty-three organizations selected for their excellence. From several hundred interviews with employees, they consolidated their findings into a list of eight critical factors or attributes that contribute to the success of organizations. Their list includes: (1) *a bias for action*—encourage creativity and be willing to risk failure; (2) *close to the customer*—have a genuine interest in meeting the needs of people; (3) *autonomy and entrepreneurship*—utilize the creativity of small work groups kept free from bureaucratic red tape; (4) *productivity through people*—treat employees like adults with high expectations, direct communication, and plenty of affirmation for achievement; (5) *hands-on, value driven*—formulate a belief system expressing clear, qualitative values; (6) *stick to the knitting*—focus on your best product, avoid getting spread too thin; (7) *simple form, lean staff*—keep the management structure simple, flexible, and stable; (8) *simultaneous loose-tight properties*—maintain the tension between creative chaos and disciplined adherence to the values.

In attribute number five, Peters and Waterman discovered seven consistent themes describing the underlying values of these organizations, including beliefs about being the "best," valuing people as individuals, and the importance of informality to enhance communication. To participate in one of these organizations is like being on a championship team, or being part of a creative and caring family, or being involved in a pioneering adventure on a new frontier. These organizations are stimulating and contagious. They generate energy rather than deplete it.

From this research on excellence, Robert Waterman turned his energies to exploring how organizations successfully encounter change. Change is the one constant that organizations face. It cannot be avoided. Only those organizations that are able to interpret what the changes will require of them and that actively manage the adjustments needed, will survive with vigor. Without this ongoing renewal, there can be no ongoing excellence. The project looked initially at five hundred companies in fifty-three industries. This field was narrowed to forty-five organizations, large and small, profit and nonprofit, which had faced the challenge of renewal successfully. The results were published in 1987 in Waterman's book *The Renewal Factor*.[3]

Successful leaders of renewal are called "builders" and are described as persons who desire to make things better in the world; and they believe that they can. Builders are contrasted with "custodians" and "manipulators." Custodians are masters of inactivity. They dislike change. Under their leadership, organizations fail to recognize the changes taking place, fail to adapt, and eventually die. The manipulators, on the other hand, are extremely active, but they place their own ends above those of the organization. Under their leadership organizations become mere gadgets in a game played by those who seek rewards only for themselves.

The behavior and personalities of the builders varied greatly, but Waterman identifies eight consistent "dynamics of renewal" that they employed as leaders. The eight dynamics of renewal are: (1) *informed opportunism*—quality information reduces the threat of surprise and enables flexible and intuitive planning; (2) *direction and empowerment*— management may establish the direction but everyone's input is valued; (3) *friendly facts, congenial controls*—contextual and factual information is welcomed because it allows decisions that anticipate change rather than just react to it; (4) *a different mirror*—habitual patterns isolate and entrench, but renewal leaders listen constantly to the best ideas available; (5) *teamwork and trust, not politics and power*—cooperation generates confidence and is more effective than competition and power politics; (6) *stability in motion*—renewal requires breaking old habits and empty patterns while maintaining stability through consistent beliefs, values, and vision; (7) *attitudes and attention*—renewal flows from attitudes and involvement that communicate attentive, confident optimism; and (8) *causes and commitment*—meaning in life emerges from a cause large enough to believe in that generates commitment by addressing human needs.

Although these studies generally are couched in the language of business and management, the issues addressed are in many ways common to any human endeavor. Turning around a struggling congregation of Christ's church is certainly more than merely renewing an organization, but it is not less. Several of the themes described as renewal and revitalization strategies for businesses and corporations, show up again in studies of revival and renewal movements in the history of the church as well as in local congregations.

17

From Church History

One of the excellent studies of renewal movements throughout church history is *Signs of the Spirit: How God Reshapes the Church* by Howard Snyder. In the introduction, Snyder reminds his readers "that every renewal movement is, in some way, linked to others in history, and that somehow both socio-cultural dynamics and the Holy Spirit are at work down through history."[4] His analysis begins with the late second century "First Charismatic Movement" or "New Prophecy Movement" later called "Montanism." The spiritual vitality and boldness of those involved challenged the authority and control of the established church. Conflict was inevitable. But conflict is almost always inevitable when the fresh wind of a turnaround movement is blowing.

Although Snyder takes a brief look at several other movements in the early centuries of the church, and offers an excellent chapter on the theory of revitalization, the larger part of his work focuses on three later movements: Pietism, Moravianism, and Methodism. Aside from his own background, part of his interest in these particular movements is that they "were movements within large established church communions. These movements did not intend to start new sects, but to revitalize the established church."[5]

By gleaning the best lessons from these earlier movements, and hoping to offer a model of renewal for our day that "brings new life to the larger church without either compromising its own validity or causing a split,"[6] Snyder concludes his work with chapter 9: "Building a Renewal Strategy for the Local Church." He writes:

> The first and perhaps most critical beginning point for renewal is to understand that the church has an inborn tendency to grow. Growth is in its genes. Whatever its pathologies, every church has a vital urge toward its own health and renewal. The reason for this is simple, and simply profound: The church is the body of Christ. The very Spirit of Jesus is at work in his church, always prodding and drawing it toward life and renewal. The key to renewal therefore is always a matter of identifying and removing the hindrances to vitality, never a matter of simply finding the right method, program, or success formula.

Since this is true, we may identify several keys to building a viable renewal strategy in local churches.[7]

Ten strategies to renew local churches are then presented as a model. (1) *Begin with life*. Recognize and affirm the life and vitality already present in both individuals and structures. (2) *Don't attack entrenched institutional patterns*. If possible, bypass them and build new relationships and structures of renewal. (3) *Seek to pastor all the people*. Even those most opposed who resist persuasive argument can often be won over by demonstrated caring. (4) *Build a balance of worship, community, and witness*. Healthy churches reveal these qualities, and healthy churches grow. (5) *Provide small groups and home meetings*. The form may vary, but small groups meeting weekly are a critical ingredient for developing commitment to serious Christian discipleship. (6) *Affirm the ministry of all believers*. Teach the priesthood of all believers, offer training in discovering and using spiritual gifts, and free all persons to be in ministry for Jesus Christ. (7) *Move toward the biblical model of leadership*. Christian leadership only grows out of discipleship. Those gifted and called to leadership are called to equip others for ministry and to function as part of a larger leadership team for the congregation. (8) *Help the congregation discover its own identity*. Pastors are key to this "conceptual renewal" that allows each congregation to discover its own unique identity and mission within the framework of the gospel of the kingdom of God. (9) *Work to ensure that financial stewardship authentically reflects the church's mission and self-identity*. Finances are connected to discipleship not to projects. God provides as we truly seek first the kingdom. (10) *Help the church catch a kingdom vision*. Although mentioned last, this is the most important. "Ongoing vitality is grounded in both the vision and the practice of consistent, continuous evangelism and compassionate, effective social transformation."[8]

As might be expected by those who have a strong creation theology, the principles discovered by Snyder and those discovered by Waterman are very similar. Notice especially how both emphasize the importance of open and visionary leadership, and the creative use of all persons' gifts. Many of these principles or strategies will be seen again as we turn now to the reports of turnaround in small churches.

Turnaround Reports from Small Churches

What do the turnaround leaders in smaller churches say are the key ingredients in bringing new life to their congregations? Their stories and descriptions of turnaround range from simple statements of faith in God to complex lists of plans and strategies; but all are marvelous reminders of God's amazing grace and available power.

Ray Barkey, pastor of the Maple Grove Church of the Brethren in New Paris, Indiana, confesses "We have done some things right and many wrong. We are a modern day example of God's miraculous grace and restoration. Like Jericho and Gideon, we don't make sense; but when God is active, who cares!"

Bob Coleman at Arnold's Chapel United Methodist Church in Bessemer, Alabama, says: "I do not understand the changes we are experiencing. We evidently are doing all the right things without being aware. Our D.S. responded when I asked for some help in leadership training, 'You should be training others!'"

As I said, some aren't sure why they are experiencing growth, they just are pleased! Most often, however, the pastors of growing and lively smaller churches have a fairly clear idea of what they are doing to be colaborers with God in bringing turnaround to their congregations.

J. R. Gonzales, pastor of the Westwood, California, Assembly of God, reports:

> This is what God did in our depressed community. When I first came, God spoke to me, and I knew God was going to turn this community around. That first year we revitalized our facilities. The second year we visited. The third year we preached and prayed harder. God directed us to prepare for the recession, and we started a food bank. This year God is telling us to prepare for a window of opportunity for future evangelism. This is how we did it, by hearing what God was and is saying.

Bob Edwards, pastor of the Judsonia United Methodist Church in Little Rock, Arkansas, writes:

> Foremost is a strong pulpit with meaningful messages. Next, I love my people and seek to meet their pastoral needs. Next, I enlist lay people in doing ministry (first in Jerusalem . . . and then to the uttermost parts of the world).

When describing the stages his congregation went through he lists the following:

1. We made some definite physical improvements—clean, paint, rearrange, and so on. 2. The pastor shared some "dreams" for the church in the next ten years. 3. We started a "Disciple" study (and bragged and let them witness). 4. We "gathered" a choir (and bragged) and then started rehearsals (and bragged some more). 5. We invited music groups from neighboring communities to sing. 6. We built a plan for young adults—new class, nursery, and quarterly parties. 7. We established a "Kids Club" Sunday evenings.

The Reverend Patty Beagle at Independence United Methodist Church in Wellsburg, West Virginia, tells the story of their resurrection from a tiny church at death's door to a church full of hope.

Four years ago the conference and district were thinking of closing this church. It was a small church sharing a pastor with a large church. The pastor just didn't feel he had time to care for this church. It was run-down and declining in attendance year after year and reached bottom at five. Three years ago they decided (upon recommendation by another pastor and a friend of the little church) to separate this 152 year old congregation from the larger church, make it a single point charge, and have it served by a part-time Local Pastor. It would either survive or die—something like pulling the plug on a patient on life support systems. I was sent to pastor this "new" charge at that time. I have been blessed to be a part of it. Independence UMC is not only surviving, but thriving and growing. Thanks be to God!

In that first year we received ten new members, had a confirmation class for eight young people and a new members celebration day, began our nursing home ministry, had potluck dinners, started special fund raisers and an "outreach jar" to send money each month to a special need or cause. This church was "The Church" this past year. Their availability enabled the Holy Spirit of God to work in and through them. Thanks be to God!

Rose Sims, in her book *The Dream Lives On*, describes a simple but amazingly effective approach for turning around small rural churches used by her husband, Oscar Grindheim. Oscar was an immigrant from Norway arriving in the United States just as the Nazi war machine landed in his homeland. Here he met and married his wife, Rose, and pursued his dream of bringing new life to dying churches all across the land. In 1966 the American Baptist Convention honored him as the "Outstanding Rural Minister in America."

21

Upon moving to Missouri, he and Rose became Methodists and continued the work of "opening church doors shut as tightly as great coffin lids, after the mourners had gone." She continues:

> Time and again, three years after Oscar had stood at a tightly barred door, that church would lead the state in professions of faith and missions. Lives were miraculously changed by his undaunted faith in the Master Builder.
>
> Then, because churches of the quality he forged were always in demand, a full-time pastor would be appointed. Once again we would be standing at a lonely, nearly forgotten, nailed-shut church door. Time and time again, over twenty-seven years, Oscar proved that renewal could happen anywhere fishermen dared to battle the elements of neglect and discouragement and put out their nets for a catch.[9]

Inspiring imagery, but how did it happen? Rose Sims records Oscar's simple seven-step formula as "hard work, prayerful vigilance, evangelistic zeal for winning the lost, powerful preaching, willing counseling, adequate and attractive buildings, and a pastor and people totally committed to Christ."[10] The "Grindheim formula" is simple and straightforward, but the strategies it represents are highly effective in bringing struggling and dying churches to new life and vitality.

Thousands of similar stories are being told in communities large and small across the land as small churches are experiencing turnaround. Our goal is to learn from these stories and the people of these churches the lessons that might encourage and instruct others who are praying and working for a story of their own.

Twelve Emerging Turnaround Strategies

From the questions asked the pastors[11] and from interviews it is possible to identify twelve critical tasks or strategies for turning around small churches. These are not listed in sequential order, but in the order deemed most important by turnaround pastors.

Turnaround Strategies for Small Churches

1. Enhance congregational confidence and hope for the future.
2. Stimulate concern for unreached persons in the community.

3. Engage in proactive and effective pastoral leadership.
4. Encourage an open, loving atmosphere in the congregation.
5. Clarify your own personal vision and be an example.
6. Help develop a clear, shared, congregational vision.
7. Work and pray for spiritual renewal among the members.
8. Provide high quality preaching and inspirational worship.
9. Lead the effort to reach new people and grow.
10. Emphasize and practice prayer.
11. Develop new programs, especially for children and youth.
12. Plan to take risks and take them.

These twelve turnaround strategies emerge again and again in various combinations as both the pastors and the members of revitalized smaller churches tell their stories. Pastors and other leaders of small congregations wishing to emerge from a season of decline and discouragement will do well to review this list carefully, and invest wholeheartedly in those areas still needing particular attention.

What's to Come?

Like it or not, it is clear that pastoral leadership is critical to the turnaround process. Therefore, chapter 2 takes a look at the pastors who make a difference. Chapter 3 explores the dynamics of bringing spiritual renewal to a congregation. Chapter 4 examines the major obstacles encountered and how they can be sidestepped or overcome. Chapter 5 looks intentionally at strategies for evangelistic outreach and church growth. The sixth chapter investigates how effective pastors lead their congregations to greater maturity in living together as Christian disciples. Chapter 7 offers a hopeful and enlightening glimpse into the kind of leadership needed to turn around churches located in communities where cultural and ethnic transitions are underway. Finally, for those who might be interested, Appendix A allows the "experts" themselves—turnaround small church pastors—to speak to seminaries and denominational leaders about the role that they can play in preparing and encouraging pastors who will make the difference.

When invited into these churches and when listening to their pastors describe how God has brought them new life, the unavoidable conclusion is that congregational turnaround is ultimately the work of the Holy Spirit. We are only privileged to play a part, but it is an important part. Yet, as colaborers with God, "neither the one who plants nor the one who waters is anything, but only God who gives the growth. . . . For we are God's servants, working together" (1 Cor. 3:7-9).

II

PASTORS AS TURNAROUND LEADERS

Are we beginning to commend ourselves again?
Surely we do not need, as some do, letters of recommen-
dation to you or from you, do we? . . . Our competence
is from God, who has made us competent to be minis-
ters of a new covenant, not of letter but of spirit; for
the letter kills, but the Spirit gives life. . . . Since, then,
we have such a hope, we act with great boldness.

2 Corinthians 3:1, 5, 12

Pastoral leadership, especially in smaller churches, is sometimes said to be much more the work of an artist than the work of a management technician. Carl Dudley proposes that "The power of the pastor stems from the pastor's willingness to walk with the congregation through the abyss, through the mysteries of life. . . . Management skills can be learned, but leadership is discovered in relationship to a group who confirm the leader with particular authority."[1] Many denominations and the pastors they ordain assume that authority is a kind of power granted by an institution, only to discover that such authority is not necessarily recognized by the congregations supposedly benefiting from these "authorized pastors." We shall see, however, that pastoral authority may not merely be something discovered or something conferred by the congregation. Leadership authority, or power for effective change, is a complex relationship between natural and spiritual gifts, personality, learned skills, and divine intervention.

The apostle Paul had his own share of difficulties in being recognized as a fully qualified and authoritative apostle in the early church. In the passage from the Corinthian letter cited above he reminds his hearers of the spiritual nature of his competence to be a minister of the new covenant. His authority is ultimately from God, who called him and equipped him by the Holy Spirit. Likewise, he writes to the church at Thessalonica: "So deeply do we care for you that we are determined to share with you not only the gospel of God but also our own selves, because you have become very dear to us" (1 Thess. 2:8).

How can skillful pastors who long for the resurrection power of God to be manifest in their churches, learn to patiently guide a congregation through all the necessary stages of change involved in turnaround? The answer is love. Love is more an art than a science. It is a matter of Spirit and not merely a matter of letter or code. It is modeled after the Master Shepherd himself, who for three years patiently walked and worked with twelve disciples who frequently struggled to understand the new message and adjust to the messenger. When Paul was at his best, he learned how to be an imitator of Christ and bring the art of love's patience to the urgency of the gospel's task.

This is the same boldness and gentleness, urgency and grace that flavor the lives of pastors identified as "turnaround leaders." They have sometimes failed, and they have been misunderstood; but they have learned from their mistakes and have been encouraged by the Spirit of God. And through it all, they have grown to love their congregations and the communities in which they serve. Other things can be said about them, but nothing more important.

Who Are the Pastors?

So who are the pastors today who make the right kind of difference in small churches and enable them to recover a sense of power

PASTORS AS TURNAROUND LEADERS

and purpose? What are their gifts and training? How are they viewed by their congregations? What are their emphases in ministry? What have they learned the hard way, by making mistakes? What are their recommendations to other pastors serving in similar congregations?

Perhaps the natural place to begin is to examine the experiences that shape their stories of being called and equipped to enter this ministry.

Personal Backgrounds

The turnaround pastors participating in this study come from all regions of the United States; however, the greatest representations are from the Northeast (29 percent), the Southeast (27 percent), the South Central (12 percent), and the Midwest (11 percent). They represent nine denominations and range in age from twenty-six to seventy with an average age of forty-seven years. Eighty-seven are men, thirteen are women. Most of them are married (90 percent) and over half (52 percent) have children living at home.

One-third of these pastors have been involved in church since birth. Ten percent did not become members of a church until after they turned eighteen. Most (61 percent) are currently serving in the same denomination they entered as members and have been pastoring for an average of fourteen years, a little over five years in their present church.

Ministry Perspectives

When asked why they had entered the ministry, overwhelmingly they responded "I was called by God" (70 percent). Other reasons for being in pastoral ministry included: "personal fulfillment" (7 percent), "to preach the gospel" (5 percent), "to love God and do God's will" (4 percent), and "to help others know God" (4 percent).

When asked to identify themselves with a theological label, they preferred terms like "evangelical," "moderate," "charismatic," or some combination of these terms rather than "fundamental," "conservative," or "liberal." They were also asked to locate themselves on a theological scale from liberal to conservative as compared to other pastors in their denomination. Although most were not fond of such simplified theological categories, 15 percent saw themselves more liberal, 21 percent saw themselves in the middle of their

27

denomination's spectrum, and 60 percent felt they were more conservative.

Almost 90 percent of these pastors record a definite conversion experience. Most felt that this experience heightened their concern for others, or encouraged them to emphasize Christian witnessing and extend evangelistic invitations. When asked "What is your motivation for being involved in evangelism?" three primary answers emerge. The first is described as an internal motivation based on the work of the Spirit and our new nature as God's children and Christ's disciples (21 percent). The second motivation is described as obedience to God's will (22 percent). The third and by far the most frequently mentioned motivation is the desire to bring to others the benefits of faith in Christ (57 percent).

Each of these motivations is clearly "Christian" and "biblical," and all three may only be facets of the same reality. Nevertheless, it is clear that most turnaround pastors prefer to describe the motivation for their task in terms of the needs of others. People who describe their motivation for evangelism this way usually define successful evangelism in terms of changed people. Persons preferring the "obedience" theme might be less concerned with "success" so long as they have been "faithful." Pastors describing their motivation as the natural outflow of God's love may resist evangelistic planning and prefer instead to leave everything to the leading of the Spirit. Perhaps additional research would show that we are looking as much at denominational doctrines as we are at individual preferences and personalities. In any case, the turnaround pastors desire changed lives and expect to see the transformation.

Preparation for Ministry

Earlier studies have indicated that full seminary education is not necessarily an indicator of effectiveness in serving smaller churches.[2] What kinds of preparation for ministry are most important when revitalized congregations are the objective?

Two-thirds of the participating pastors completed an M.Div. degree as part of their theological education. Forty-one seminaries were named, including institutions where denominational courses of study were pursued instead of academic degrees. Sixty-two percent of these pastors indicated that they had little or no training in evangelism prior to pursuing their formal theological education. But the reverse of this statistic is that 38 percent indicated they had some or much training in evangelism prior to beginning their theological work. Fifty percent indicated they received no seminary course work in evangelism or church growth. Nevertheless, those who did have such courses ranked them as the most helpful for their ministry. Likewise, evangelism and church growth courses topped all lists for seminary classes most needed.

More will be said about the perspectives of these pastors on formal theological education in Appendix A. It is obvious, however, that turnaround pastors are committed to "continuing education." Ninety-three percent indicate they take advantage of "other" training opportunities and read widely to enhance their ministry effectiveness.

What Pastoral Gifts and Skills Are Needed?

Nearly every book written on ministry related to the small church emphasizes that the relational skills are most important. The small church sometimes has been compared to a tribe[3] and other times to a family.[4] In both cases the importance of the image employed is to remind pastors and other small church leaders of the human dynamics and decision-making processes utilized by families and tribes. These smaller and more intimate social institutions function quite differently from larger and more formal ones.

As a young pastor unfamiliar with these dynamics, this author almost drove himself and his congregation crazy trying to "run" a small church the way he had learned in seminary and in larger churches. Resources on small churches produced in the 1970s and 1980s were enormously helpful to many of us pastoring at that time. The purpose of this particular section is to identify the special gifts and skills of pastors today who are successfully leading smaller churches into new life and growth. Some "gifts and graces" for pastoral ministry are the same no matter where one serves. Others, however, seem to be uniquely important for effective ministry in smaller congregations.

When the pastors identify and rank their own strongest qualities and skills for ministry, their top twelve answers are:

Gifts and Skills for Ministry

1. Preaching
2. Loving people
3. Skills in working with people
4. Administration and organization
5. Teaching and training
6. Being a visionary and motivating people
7. Visitation one-on-one
8. Counseling
9. Leading by example
10. Faith and loving God
11. Evangelism
12. An energetic, hard worker

What kind of composite profile might emerge from this list? Pastors successfully leading small churches into new life and effective ministries of outreach and evangelism are excited about and feel competent in announcing good news from their pulpits. They love and understand people, and are comfortable with the patient task of building trusting relationships through affirmation, encouragement, challenge, confrontation, and good communication. They also like a sense of order and momentum. They see personal relationships as the foundation of the small church, but not the only concern. They work hard and feel comfortable making decisions needed for the day-to-day and the long-range coordination of church programs and ministries. They especially like to sense that others are catching a new vision of the meaning of the gospel for their daily living, and enjoy both teaching biblical perspectives and training people in ways to invest this information.

Turnaround pastors know that people need a sense of how to see and shape their future. These good shepherds confidently lead the way to greener pastures. They do not, however, neglect to care for each member of their flock. They visit them in their homes, offer counsel, and pray for them in times of trouble. They also reach out beyond the existing congregation to offer these manifestations of God's love and our hope in Christ to others. They are not going to ask others in the congregation to do things they are unwilling to do themselves. New life always means change, and change means taking risks. A deep sense of confident faith in the Lord, whose love and guiding presence is the same "yesterday, today, and forever," inspires them to move ahead no matter what obstacles may stand in the way. They have a contagious spirit of hope and endurance that does not falter even in times of disappointment because of their trust in the presence of the Holy Spirit.

Does this all sound a bit ideal? Perhaps it is, but the congregations served by these pastors are themselves living witnesses to this contagious life. Four of the churches visited as part of this study encouraged members to share their own observations of the changes in their church and the role their pastors played. Surveys were handed out to those willing to take a few minutes to share their ideas. One question asked "What are your pastor's three greatest assets and strengths in ministry?" According to their members, the greatest "assets and strengths" of their pastors are:

How Members Rank Their Pastors' Gifts

1. Loving people
2. People skills
3. Preaching
4. Visionary and motivator
5. Personal faith and love of God

Also mentioned as important in approximately equal numbers, although less frequently than the above list, were the following:

- Leader by example
- Teaching and training
- Evangelism
- Hard work, commitment, and enthusiasm
- Administration and organization

It is clear that the "gifts and skills" of turnaround pastors that are most noticed and valued by their members are in line with the pastors' self-evaluations, namely: (1) loving and working skillfully with people, (2) preaching alive and meaningful messages from the Bible, and (3) modeling a personal faith and offering a vision of hope. These are the personal contributions that form the core of the pastoral

31

leadership that enables endangered smaller churches to recover their sense of importance and effectively engage their communities with an alive and powerful Christian witness.

How Do Turnaround Pastors Lead?

Although these pastors lead from love, they do lead. They are not just lovers. Or to say it another way, they do not value relationships and peaceful unity to the point that they will avoid conflict at all costs. They seem to be well aware that positive change demands the risk of initiative. These pastors list a congregational atmosphere of "love and acceptance" as the most important growth factor for their churches. But in second place they list "pastoral initiative." Or to put it another way, they say that one of the most important factors impeding turnaround is, simply put, "pastors who don't lead." Pastors must lead if churches are to change.

There are today a multitude of models being offered as the true and most effective definitions and descriptions of leadership, both for the church and for secular institutions. The church has cycled through the nondirective "facilitator" and "counselor" models of the 1950s and 1960s, and the "servant" and "equipper" models of the 1970s and 1980s, to the "spiritual leader," "change agent," and "team builder" models of the 1990s. And always in the background have been the models of "shepherd," "herald," "priest," "prophet," and even "king." How do the pastors in our study define their leadership?

When asked to portray the leadership role and approach they employed for revitalization and growth, most offered multiple descriptions of their efforts. For example, one pastor said "visionary and catalyst as well as administrator." Another answered "stabilizer, teacher, observer, exhorter." They seemed uncomfortable using any single term to define their pastoral leadership. Of the twenty-one categories identified, however, their top eleven answers are:

Leadership Role of the Pastor

1. Visionary
2. Enabler/Encourager
3. Partner/Friend

4. Facilitator
5. Cheerleader
6. Transformational Leader/Change Agent
7. Spiritual Leader
8. Caregiver
9. Manager/Director
10. Coach for Success
11. Expert/Initiator

In reality "visionary" stands significantly above the others, receiving a third more votes than "Enabler/Encourager," and twice as many as "Partner/Friend." Whatever else these pastors do, they bring with them and plant in the hearts and minds of their congregations a vision of what can be.

Whether or not these pastors are familiar with the work of Warren Bennis and Burt Nanus on leaders, they manifest in their leadership much the same style these two researchers found after interviewing ninety outstanding CEOs and leaders in the public sector. Bennis and Nanus write:

> The study pursued leaders who have achieved fortunate mastery over present confusion—in contrast to those who simply react, throw up their hands, and live in a perpetual state of "present shock."
>
> The problem with many organizations, and especially the ones that are failing, is that they tend to be overmanaged and underled. They may excel in the ability to handle the daily routine, yet never question whether the routine should be done at all. There is a profound difference between management and leadership, and both are important. "To manage" means "to bring about, to accomplish, to have charge of or responsibility for, to conduct." "Leading" is "influencing, guiding in direction, course, action, opinion." The distinction is crucial. *Managers are people who do things right and leaders are people who do the right thing.* The difference may be summarized as activities of vision and judgment—*effectiveness*, versus activities of mastering routines—*efficiency*.[5]

Pastoral leadership, like any other kind of *effective* leadership, requires initiative that has a direction, a goal, a vision of what God wants to do and will do among us. For Jesus, the dominant motif was the establishment of the kingdom of God. What are the biblical images or themes most helpful to motivate and energize turnaround pastors? Each pastor was given the option of listing up to three such vision-inspiring resources. The result is 94 different favorites out of 230 votes cast. Those mentioned most frequently are listed below along with the number of votes they received.

Biblical Sources for Pastoral Vision

1. The Great Commission—Matt. 28:16-20 (27)
2. The Body of Christ—Eph. 4:7-16 (14)
3. Abundant life and the Good Shepherd—John 10:1-18 (11)
4. Pentecost—Acts 2:1-47 (10)
5. New birth and God's gift in Christ—John 3:1-17 (10)
6. God's activity in the early church—Acts (9)
7. Seeking and receiving the lost—Luke 15 (7)
8. Talents, and "unto the least of these"—Matt. 25:14-46 (6)
9. Sermon on the Mount—Matt. 5-7 (5)
10. The work of the Spirit to make us witnesses—Acts 1:8 (5)

Some authors have observed that we have largely abandoned Jesus' own vision of the kingdom of God.[6] On the other hand, some would contend that facets of the kingdom of God are embodied, even if not mentioned, in each of these other images. Some believe both sides of this argument and are working to help churches cultivate once again the great richness and power found in the holistic vision of the kingdom of God.[7] In summary it might be said that the pastors surveyed have the following vision: the Holy Spirit is present in the church enabling all to sense they have a part in extending the abundant and new life brought by Jesus Christ to a world needing to be reached with a gospel that makes them Christian disciples.

What Are Their Pastor-to-Pastor Suggestions?

Our turnaround pastors were asked what suggestions they would offer to other pastors of smaller churches who were interested in evangelism and church growth. Their top twenty collegial recommendations are:

Their Recommendations to Other Pastors
1. Know and love your people.
2. Preach the wonderful gospel of Christ.

34

3. Pray and enable your people to pray.
4. Help your people reach out to others.
5. Help them dream of what they can be for God's glory.
6. Work hard; nothing comes easy.
7. Accept yourself and your people and "press on."
8. Be patient; new life grows slowly.
9. Hold on to and hold out your vision.
10. Celebrate the good that is happening.
11. Go ahead and risk new ideas and new programs.
12. Know and love God.
13. Teach God's purpose as found in the Bible.
14. Train people in evangelism and church growth.
15. Get yourself and others out visiting.
16. Take key people with you to training events.
17. Start with a committed core, don't wait for everyone.
18. Read about and study small churches that grow.
19. Set goals and move toward a strategic plan.
20. Delegate all you can and enlist new people.

These recommendations are not exactly steps, stages, or "the two-times-ten commandments" for congregational turnaround, but they do reveal once more how the twelve strategies mentioned in chapter 1 reappear in various forms as turnaround pastors share their hearts with colleagues committed to the same cause.

Learning from Mistakes

To meet and talk with these pastors makes it clear that they are not all cut from the same cloth, nor do they make everyone happy. Of course, neither did Jesus, or Peter, or Paul, or Augustine, or Aquinas, or Francis, or Luther, or Susanna Wesley, or the most popular previous pastor. Making decisions and moving ahead is risky. Change means that disagreements will emerge. Feelings will be hurt. The definition and possession of power and influence will shift. Mistakes will be made by pastors as well as by parishioners.

When they were asked "What mistakes have you made that have become 'lessons the hard way'?" their answers varied from "None that I can think of" to "So many I can hardly believe it." However, in

God's grace these brothers and sisters indicate they are learning to accept their own human faults and frailties without being immobilized by them. Perhaps knowing ourselves in this way is the first step to being able to handle gracefully the problems that occur when others don't readily and wisely respond to our leadership. Another important "people skill" occasionally listed by the pastors as well as their members was a sense of humor. To be able to laugh at ourselves in those inevitable times of error or embarrassment is often the critical keystone needed to complete the doorway of trust and freedom that we must all walk through if we are to forge ahead into a new future instead of remaining behind in isolation and fear.

So what lessons did these pastors learn the hard way? What does their confessional list of "mistakes" look like? Their top fifteen are:

Lessons Learned Through Mistakes
1. I tried to do too much alone.
2. I was impatient.
3. I believed they would follow me before they claimed the vision.
4. I made decisions without waiting for the congregation.
5. I forced my vision rather than helping them discover their own.
6. I offered inadequate or no job training.
7. I overworked the dedicated few instead of reducing the pace or recruiting more widely.
8. I allowed myself to get negative and focus on the failures.
9. I misunderstood the meaning of members' actions and/or words.
10. I ignored the reality of original sin.
11. I didn't address problems or confront problem people early enough.
12. I ignored prayer and the comfort and guidance of the Spirit.
13. I took other people's anger too personally.
14. I didn't pay enough attention to visitation and follow-up.
15. I tried to please everybody.

Some of these "mistakes" may be just part of being human—an interesting risk God took in the incarnation of Jesus. But notice that "timing" occurs as an issue in several of the items above. Generally, the pastors were of the opinion that they "rushed" things and moved ahead too soon without adequate preparation, training, or ownership by the congregation. However, they also realized that they were caught in a predicament. There seemed to be no "perfect" time to move. Resistance never completely disappeared. One pastor acknowledged that just as soon as the congregation was over the last "fight" and was celebrating a victory, a new issue would arise and the tensions and questions would emerge again.

On the other hand, creative and energetic pastors are well counseled to be aware of their tendency to be impatient. Their own sense of satisfaction and success is usually tied to the changes they are working for in accord with the vision they have for the congregation's future. But timing and patience are much more important in small congregations than in large ones, and listening to the pulse of the congregation ought to be the job of the many and not just the one. It is a mistake to go it alone, trusting only one's own intuitions without checking with several honest friends in the church, including some who might disagree.

The goal is not to win battles or wars, but to enable a congregation to move as united as possible into its own new future. R. Robert Cueni has two extremely practical resources written for pastors. *The Vital Church Leader* appears as an earlier volume in the Effective Church Series edited by Herb Miller. In a previous book, *What Ministers Can't Learn in Seminary*, Cueni offers helpful wisdom on how to avoid a number of traps as ministers move away from their formal training into the world of the pastorate. Commenting on how to define "success" he writes:

> The church's primary concern remains the cure of souls, not management by objectives. When we are more concerned with meeting goals than caring for people, we have forgotten what it means to be the church.
>
> It is, of course, important to keep measurable goals before the church. The church growth movement ably points to scriptural comments on the numbers of people joining the church. We deceive ourselves when we say we are concerned about people but fail to discuss numerical goals for the people we want to reach, the money we seek to raise, the programs we want to conduct, or the buildings we plan to build. . . . We must not, however, mistake the ends for the means. . . . The success of any congregation or pastor should be

determined by what happens in the lives of those who are being touched by congregation and pastor.[8]

It took Jesus three years of ministry with a very small band of believers to know the right timing from his Father for his ultimate investment in the cure of souls. He often asked "How much longer?" but until he had that answer, he demonstrated patient consistency. Pastors need to press on toward the mark of their high calling, but always with the cure of souls as their goal, and always with these words at work as a healing balm for their own souls.

Love is patient; love is kind; love is not envious or boastful or arrogant or rude. It does not insist on its own way; it is not irritable or resentful; it does not rejoice in wrongdoing, but rejoices in the truth. It bears all things, believes all things, hopes all things, endures all things. (1 Cor. 13:4-7)

To the Turnaround

Pastoral leadership in smaller congregations is more an art than a science. We need to avoid the pitfalls and heed the time lines. But all these lessons are best learned by those who love what they are doing, love the One who called them into this crazy and challenging vocation, and love the very human brothers and sisters they work with for the glory of God's kingdom.

One of the important skills essential to effective turnaround leadership is knowing where the congregation is in relation to where it has been and where it is going. Several writers have addressed the stages or seasons of ministry in smaller churches. James Cushman, who now works for small church revitalization out of the national offices of the Presbyterian Church U.S.A. in Louisville, Kentucky, describes three stages of pastoral acceptance and leadership. The first stage focuses on establishing the primary relationship between the pastor and the people. He calls this the community acceptance stage. The second stage he describes as the season of fulfilling pastoral functions. Here the pastor is accepted by most of the people as their preacher, teacher, and counselor and is free to function well in these areas. This is the time to begin working creatively for program planning and development. The third stage begins when the pastor is accepted as a full community participant, as much a part of the larger community as anyone else. This normally comes as the congregation is extending its mission intentionally into the community. This progression of pastoral acceptance and leadership authority often takes five to seven years in Cushman's experience.[9]

Rene O. Bideaux, a former director of the Hinton Rural Life Center, suggests that there are four developmental stages that smaller churches and their pastors go through in moving from "disconnectedness to interdependence, from dormancy to vitality, from death to life, from decline to growth."[10] He observes a shorter time line than Cushman, but still agrees that just getting from stage one—"Disconnected," to stage four—"Interdependent or Mutual," can take as long as four years.

We will examine more closely the idea of stages of change in the next chapter as we explore the processes involved in leading a congregation to "turn toward the Spirit," a turning that is critical if a church is to find a new sense of faith, power, and confidence.

III
TURNING TOWARD THE SPIRIT

*Take care, or you will be seduced into turning away,
serving other gods and worshiping them, for then the
anger of the LORD will be kindled against you and he
will shut up the heavens . . . and the land will yield no
fruit; then you will perish quickly.*
                                        Deuteronomy 11:16-17

*You foolish Galatians! Who has bewitched you? . . .
Having started with the Spirit, are you now ending with
the flesh? Did you experience so much for nothing?*
                                        Galatians 3:1, 3-4

A Look at the Problem

It is not a new problem for the people of God to turn away from the Spirit and ignore the counsel of God. Probably each of us knows the problem personally, as well as having noted the evidence of turning away in congregations and entire denominations. Through the centuries God has sent prophets, apostles, reformers, and has even come himself in Jesus to call us back to our "first love" and rekindle the flame of the Holy Spirit in our midst. It is clear, however, that the established religious people who thought of themselves as on God's side, frequently did not respond well to the voices of these messengers. Thus, leaders today with similar goals in mind ought not be surprised if their voices are not immediately welcomed by all who hear.

The early church, even in the days of wonderful, pentecostal freshness, had to face the problem again and again. As early as the fifth chapter of Acts, Ananias and Sapphira demonstrate how easy it is to "play along" without truly being committed to the vision or sensitive to the presence of the Spirit. Peter had to confront them and remind the whole church of the dangers of lying to God and living a double-minded life—as James later called it. In fact, both New and Old Testaments are filled with very similar counsel and correction.

Were it not for trouble in the churches that Peter and Paul founded, we would have a very small New Testament, if we had any at all. So it could be said that churches struggling with strife, party-spirit, spiritual coldness, loss of love for widows and orphans, lack of courage, no desire to risk the dangers of bearing witness, and immorality in all its forms are in good company and merely part of that great line of splendor. Church work, and the work of the church, both demand that we face squarely the reality that although sin and death have been defeated through Christ's death and resurrection, they both are the source still of the decay and decline that induce our inertia.

All the problems faced by churches, especially today's smaller congregations, however, cannot be easily traced to such traditional understandings of sin. Many kinds of changes have taken their toll through the years. Most smaller congregations in the United States are located in rural areas and small towns. Economic and social shifts during the past half-century have not been particularly beneficial to these communities. Many communities have experienced significant population loss or radical shifts in ethnic and cultural makeup. Most often, the old mainline denominations have declined in both members and congregations while independent and nonmainline churches have not declined as quickly. The cost of supporting a pastor's family has risen dramatically. One study of smaller churches in Missouri published in 1988 indicated that 43 percent of rural congregations in that state were spending more than 50 percent of their budget simply to support a pastor.[1] In addition, the problem of frequent pastoral changes has denied smaller churches the continuity of leadership so important to long-term church growth.

Smaller, rural institutions of all types have suffered losses throughout this century. Schools, banks, businesses, and even family farms have been forced into consolidation. Historic smaller towns all over the country have boarded up most of what is left of their "downtowns." It is a miracle that most of the churches in these communities have survived at all when so many institutions around them have collapsed, closed down, or consolidated. No wonder the number one ailment of smaller congregations today, according to many studies, is the problem of "low self-esteem." In fact, by an almost two-to-one margin, pastors confirm that negative self-image is the number one problem facing smaller churches.

A survey of lay persons in The United Methodist Church highlights another side of this social and spiritual malaise. Clark Morphew, an ordained minister and regular columnist for the *St. Paul* (Minnesota) *Pioneer Press*, writes:

> Only 3 percent of respondents said they want their pastor to have the following positive characteristics: competence, independence, determination, courageousness, maturity, fair-mindedness, dependability, forward-looking attitude, imagination and ambition.
>
> More than 40 percent of those taking the survey said they want their pastor to be cooperative, caring, and honest. Those are all good characteristics to have if clergy are simply expected to maintain the status quo.
>
> But if clergy also are expected to drive the congregation's mission forward or shape public opinion or make the church grow, there had better be some courage in the preacher's soul.
>
> I fear for these old churches as they plod toward tomorrow, having already accepted that they are dying. What, I wonder, can awaken them from this self-induced slumber?[2]

Morphew believes that this discontinuity explains much of today's conflict between parishioners and clergy.

The problem of conflict will be examined along with other obstacles along the turnaround path in chapter 4. But for now, the issue is the larger challenge of what a pastor can do to help shift the tide from helplessness and hopelessness to courage, empowerment, imagination, and confidence—no small task. In fact, the change must be supernatural. Turnaround pastors are quick to affirm that they do not produce this change; rather, they lead their congregations into the presence of the risen Christ and pray and wait for the Holy Spirit once more to transform struggling and defeated disciples into men and women of radiant hope.

Turning to the Spirit

In his book, *Signs of the Spirit,* Howard Snyder gleans the ages of history for principles of church renewal and revitalization. He suggests that five different, but interrelated, dimensions of renewal are important if new life is to come to a church.

1. Personal Renewal—a dramatic, decisive experience or simply a deepening that gives greater peace and joy. . . . Nothing can substitute for this. First through the new birth, then through the deepening work of the Holy Spirit, God wants every son and daughter of his to know the joy of deep, fulfilling communion with himself.

2. Corporate Renewal—a dramatic spirit of revival sweeping the church, or simply by a gentle quickening of the church's life. . . . A renewed congregation is more powerful in God's hands than a collection of isolated Christians.

3. Conceptual Renewal—God gives a new vision of what the church can and should be. . . . Conceptual renewal comes when our models are challenged, and we are forced to rethink what the church is really all about.

4. Structural Renewal—simply finding the best forms, in our day and age, for living out the new life in Christ. . . . *Any* traditional form, structure, or practice that helps us be alive and faithful should be kept and improved. Any that insulate us from the fresh fire of the Spirit should be modified or retired.

5. Missiological Renewal—A church needing renewal is focused inward. A renewed church focuses outward to mission and service in the world. . . . Sometimes renewal actually begins here.[3]

Snyder acknowledges that new life may begin in any of these five

43

areas; but for it to be long-lasting, faithful to God's purpose for the church, and dynamic, it must integrate all five dimensions.

Turnaround pastors engage in a vast array of personal and programmatic efforts to assist their congregations in the process of drawing near to God and letting God draw near to them. But six important ministry arenas can be identified that contribute significantly to Snyder's five dimensions of congregational renewal. The six renewal arenas are: (1) personal pastoral effort, (2) prayer, (3) special events and spiritual retreats, (4) Sunday worship and preaching, (5) small groups, and (6) community involvement.

1. Personal Pastoral Effort

In the last chapter we learned of the special love reported by these pastors for their people. Love does not work well from long distance or in the safety of isolation. The very heart of the good news of Jesus Christ in the doctrine of the Incarnation is that "God so loved the world that he gave his only Son" (John 3:16); and this Son so loved that he gave "his life a ransom for many" (Mark 10:45). Jesus repeatedly sought to prepare his followers for ministry in his name by reminding them what good shepherds do (Luke 15:1-7; John 10:1-18) and how to function as loving servants (John 13). Any pastor unwilling to be such a shepherd-servant is in danger not only of vocational failure, but also of God's judgment.

> Therefore, you shepherds, hear the word of the LORD: As I live, says the Lord GOD, because my sheep have become a prey, and my sheep have become food for all the wild animals, since there was no shepherd; and because my shepherds have not searched for my sheep, but the shepherds have fed themselves, and have not fed my sheep; therefore, you shepherds, hear the word of the LORD: Thus says the Lord GOD, I am against the shepherds. (Ezek. 34:7-10)

Pastors who lead their flocks like good shepherds do not see their work as a way to make a living, but rather as a way to joyfully offer up their lives in service to God and God's sheep—both the ones already gathered and those in need of being sought out and brought home. It is appropriate then that pastors who lead their congregations to turnaround offer as their number one suggestion to other shepherds of smaller flocks, "know and love your people."

In practical terms, what does this look like, and how does it contribute to congregational renewal? For one thing, it means these pastors "stay." One member of a revitalized congregation in Pennsylvania when asked what his pastor did to help it happen simply answered "He stayed! He stuck it out. The last two or three just couldn't take it and they left." I asked, "What is the 'it' they couldn't take?" He replied, "You know, the pressure: not having everything the way they wanted, people not agreeing with them, just the stuff you'd have at any church." Good shepherds have thick skin, but tender hearts and gentle hands. They aren't easily discouraged, they sense God's call to the particular parish they are serving, and they plan to stay for as long as it takes. For many of them this has meant sacrifice, and there is always the danger of self-pity. But for those who "stick it out" with joyful hearts and confidence in God's guidance, there is the wonderful reward of seeing miracles of *personal renewal* in the lives of others and *corporate renewal* for an entire congregation.

A second aspect of their pastoral care is that they pay attention to people and help them believe they are important. They "visit, visit, visit" as one pastor said when asked for suggestions he would offer to other pastors. They encourage persons during times of stress and pain, but also as a way to invite them to risk trying things they haven't done before. They know how to say "Thank you!" and "Great job!" and "Sure you can!" They send notes, stop by, and make phone calls. Members of these churches say things about their pastors like "She's warm, welcoming, knows you are there, and is fun to be with." and "You always feel like you are important to him, but then so is everyone else, too." And these pastors seem to know how to find new and important things for people to do. One fairly shy young woman was discovered to have a great love for children and artistic skills. The pastor encouraged and worked with her until she was willing to try the Sunday morning children's sermon. Eventually she created an entire illustrated book of messages for children and submitted it for publication. Recognizing, affirming, and employing for God's glory the gifts and graces of others is a critical first level ingredient in establishing a sense of hope and potential for a congregation's future. Discovering and employing people's gifts in ministry not only changes their personal lives, but frequently contributes to *conceptual, structural,* and even *missiological renewal* for the entire congregation.

A third important ingredient for renewal through personal pastoral effort is a life that reveals both spiritual spontaneity and discipline. These pastors read, study, pray, and work hard; yet they know how to prioritize needs with their families and take time off. Although they are patient about the timing of renewal, they are constantly exuding confidence that God is already at work bringing it to pass. They seem to have a twinkle in their eye, as though they know that a secret surprise party is just about to break on the scene. However, their reservoir of personal spiritual vitality is not a secret, and they let people know that they are dependent on the living water drawn from the well that never runs dry. They make time for soaking in the pages of the Bible, and they take days away on personal spiritual retreat just to walk, pray, ponder, and listen. Many of them take time every week to announce that they will be in the sanctuary praying for the needs of the congregation and the community. Some invite others to join them for these times, but only if they come to pray. Although they have plenty of new ideas because of their reading and research, they don't simply try to reproduce someone else's program. This can be and frequently is disastrous. Instead, they seem to talk about, pray about, and preach about the unique "new thing God wants to do right here with us." *Conceptual renewal* catches fire in turnaround churches because the wind of the Spirit fans the sparks of expectation struck by their pastors.

There is no way around it. Pastors are onstage and being watched as a kind of preview to the main event. As time goes by, other kindred souls will emerge with the same twinkle in their eye, or at least a hunger for it. These often form the initial informal network of support for the pastor; and like the firstfruits of springtime, reveal a foretaste of the harvest to come. One pastor revealed just such confidence when he said: "Most small churches have much more to offer the world than they think they do; and if I can awaken the spirit of even a few in a small church, it makes a big difference."

Personal pastoral effort establishes the spiritual climate and "culture" in which renewal can grow. The busy activities of *personal, corporate, conceptual, structural,* and *missiological renewal* all need a kind of peaceful center. The shepherd is not that peaceful

46

center, but he or she must point to it and live in it, or renewal has little chance of becoming a reality. Like it or not, pastors are important; and their personal effort as caring, loving, freeing, exploring, praying, praising people sounds the trumpet that God has come to meet us.

2. Prayer

Prayer is usually the starting point for *personal renewal* for members of the congregation just as it is for the pastor. Jesus carefully reminded his disciples of the image of the vine and the branches: "Just as the branch cannot bear fruit by itself unless it abides in the vine, neither can you unless you abide in me" (John 15:4). Most of us have a tendency to think that this means something like "keep believing and keep working." But it really is much more like "stay connected to me as I have stayed connected to my Father." The vine and branch image reminds us that "fruit" is what God produces, for we only bear it on God's behalf. Living the Christian life and being productive for God are not things we do. It is what the Spirit does in us as we first and foremost keep our lives connected. How? One way is through faithful attentiveness in prayer.

Prayer opens the windows of the soul. Prayer acknowledges that God alone is able. Prayer is not what we do when we've already done all that we could. Prayer is living constantly in the awareness that it is "not by might, nor by power, but by my spirit, says the LORD of hosts" (Zech. 4:6). Prayer links us to God's active presence. How can there be any personal or corporate spiritual renewal without prayer? According to most of the pastors surveyed, there can't be.

One of the most amazing stories of corporate spiritual renewal and growth is the story of Union Chapel United Methodist Church in Muncie, Indiana. This 117-year-old congregation moved twice in ten years in order to find enough space for the multitudes who have come to participate in its ministries. In 1983 worship attendance averaged seventy-eight. Today, almost fifteen hundred people are worshiping regularly in a renovated automobile showroom. Gregg Parris, the pastor, has many gifts for ministry. The members of the congregation affirm his personal integrity, his preaching, and his teaching. But most evident in their descriptions of what has changed is that Gregg has called them to prayer. One member comments:

Two years ago, Gregg challenged those worshiping regularly at Union Chapel to spend at least five minutes a day in prayer. During the past year, the emphasis on prayer has increased dramatically. Teaching a lengthy series on "How to Pray," Gregg began spending a minimum of one hour daily in prayer himself, then encouraged the rest of us to join in that commitment. It has changed lives, and our church will never be the same.

Prayer is not only a channel for *personal* and *corporate renewal*, it also contributes significantly to *conceptual* and *missiological renewal*. Bandana is a small farming community tucked away in the fertile bottomlands of the Ohio River in western Kentucky. The members of Bandana United Methodist Church lamented their declining attendance and decided to send representatives to a countywide training event on evangelism and church growth. Their pastor, Don Jones, writes:

The next week we held our own church growth meeting. We discussed each of the recommendations of the earlier meeting. One by one we ruled them out because we felt they didn't fit our situation. Since we didn't know what to do to bring about spiritual renewal, we decided to pray for guidance. The seven people at that meeting decided to challenge the congregation. To our surprise, eighteen people committed to come to the church and pray. So, we prayed for a month, coming to the church at all hours.

The first result of the prayers was this: People noticed a change in themselves. One member got up in our Sunday school assembly and said, "I've never prayed for thirty minutes at one time. And I want to tell you, it's changed my life." The second result was a change in the direction of our program planning. It seemed that several ideas became right for us. At some point, it began to dawn on us that the Holy Spirit was helping us. Ideas began to come and we didn't begrudge the extra time spent at another meeting at church. And when we started to implement these early ideas, we found continual help. People appeared out of the woodwork. We are convinced that the foundation of revival lies in seeking the guidance of the Holy Spirit through prayer.

Perhaps prayer relates to *structural renewal* only in the sense that "form" is supposed to follow "function." Once a congregation discovers a new purpose or "function," it needs new ways to organize in order to accomplish the required ministry. Small groups demand small group leaders. Mission teams require coordinators. A new choir, a second worship service, or a community-wide ecumenical food pantry often require *structural renewal* if the vision is to become reality. The early church discovered this in Acts 6:1-6 when seven new "deacons" were added to the apostolic leadership in order to care for a whole group of neglected believers.

Few in our churches today realize the missiological dimension of prayer. Prayer is a ministry of its own. One of the most unusual and effective models of *missiological renewal* through prayer comes from the Linda Vista Presbyterian Church in San Diego, California. After a merger effort with a Korean congregation failed, this small church, led by retired Air Force chaplain Richard Hayward, invested what they had been learning about prayer into a community outreach program called DIAL HOPE. Twenty-four hours a day, upwards of five thousand calls a year come in to the DIAL HOPE telephone answering machines at the church. Those who call during the week receive a prerecorded daily devotional, and on Sundays, a recorded sermon is featured. The callers are invited to request prayers for particular needs. A Discovery Prayer Group, as well as the entire congregation, prays for the requests, which are printed every Sunday in the bulletin. The Reverend Hayward writes:

> The program works. *It reaches people who need our Lord.* . . . You reach handicapped people, troubled people, people living far from your church, working people and retired people, elderly people and others who are confined and need the Word of God to uplift them. . . . And although the Dial Hope program is an outreach program, we have found it helps not only those in need but church members as well. It has stimulated Linda Vista members to witness for their Lord.[4]

This is not the only outreach program of the Linda Vista church, but it is the one that best identifies them as a congregation that trusts in God and cares about the needs of all people. Surely such an identity is close to the heart of being "turned around."

3. Special Events and Spiritual Retreats

The importance of special evangelistic events and programs does not rate as high among turnaround pastors in small churches, as some might expect. Only six of the one hundred pastors report using revivals or other special evangelistic events to reach unchurched persons in the community. More to the point, however, is how often both the members and the pastors affirm a special event as important to their personal renewal.

Some pastors arranged for a gifted colleague or evangelist to come lead a revival. Others preached their own. But what they accomplish is designed from the outset to be a "turnaround" for the believers in the congregation, not for the unchurched. The importance of prayer in the story of Union Chapel in Muncie, Indiana, was mentioned earlier; but the start of their revival is recorded in an article written to help newcomers identify the turnaround point of God's activity in their midst.

> Our church's story of renewal began several years before June of 1981, when a few prayer warriors began to pray for a Spirit-filled pastor to be appointed to what was at that time the two-point charge of Union Chapel-Millgrove, Muncie District, North Indiana Conference. The churches had a series of student pastors, and others in transition. Attendance and interest were down at the little brick structure in the middle of a cornfield about five miles from the small communities of Eaton, Dunkirk, and Albany. Gregg and Beth Parris accepted the appointment to this two-point charge in June, 1981, and moved into the parsonage with their two-year-old son, Aaron. Gregg, a 1980 graduate of Asbury Theological Seminary, began to preach the Gospel to about 80 folks at Union Chapel who showed up on that first Sunday to see what the new minister had to say. The reception Gregg and Beth received at Union Chapel was warm.
>
> In October of 1981, revival services were planned. Rev. Mark Beeson, a fellow United Methodist pastor and good friend of Parris, was scheduled to preach four nights. The services were sparsely attended, but those who were there enjoyed the spirited preaching and felt God's presence. On Thursday night, Beeson had another commitment, and Gregg preached the revival service. At the end of the service, revival broke out, with people confessing their faults, asking each other's forgiveness, and the Holy Spirit began to move in a mighty way. That revival is ongoing to this day!

There seems to be an understanding among these pastors that God often uses special events and special witnessing and preaching to stir the coals of a congregation into a rekindled fire. In addition to such stories about traditional (at least in some parts of the country) revivals and preaching missions, it is interesting to note the continuing influence of the Lay Witness Mission movement, and the arrival of a program called by various names but most commonly mentioned as The Walk to Emmaus. Seven pastors wrote about this special retreat program in their reports, and others mentioned it in conversation over the phone or in person. One pastor has more than half of his congregation involved in this renewal movement sponsored by The Upper Room in Nashville, Tennessee.[5] The kind of relational intimacy established in this spiritual formation journey is particularly appealing to small churches.

The model originated in Catholic parishes in Spain in the late 1940s. It began to make its way into Protestant circles in the United States in the 1960s and 1970s. By the early 1980s, The Upper Room in Nashville had developed its own ecumenical version and named it The Walk to Emmaus after the image of downcast disciples walking blindly with the risen Lord to Emmaus until their hearts were strangely warmed and their eyes were opened as he broke the bread (Luke 24). Men and women attend separate weekends (Thursday night to Sunday night), where they are led by a team of about twenty lay persons and clergy, usually representing several churches and denominations, through an intensive seventy-two-hour reminder of the basic ingredients of living in Christ. Outstanding music, excellent food, inspiring talks on grace and Christian living, engaging small group discussion, times of prayer, communion, and other acts of worship and reflection round out the weekend. A great variety of renewing experiences are reported by those who have attended. The stated purpose is to be an instrument of the larger church to assist local congregations in the development of Christian leaders. The primary approach, however, is not what would normally be called "leadership training." Rather, it is an experience of immersion into a community of grace where Christian essentials are rehearsed and new visions of the kingdom of God and the renewing love of the Holy Spirit are offered.

Pastors who are willing to open themselves to such special events and encourage their members to become involved, find that people revitalized in the loving grace of God want to do something about it. They want others to experience what they have. They want to offer

51

themselves in sacrificial service to others. Larry Frank, pastor of a church in Conestoga, Pennsylvania tells of the man in his congregation who returned from an Emmaus weekend and said "What job do you need done that nobody else wants to do?" Larry Frank answered, "Mow the lawn in the cemetery." Then he adds, "It's looked like a green patch of heaven ever since!"

Special events and programs of spiritual challenge and refreshment can play a significant role in the process of renewing a congregation. Wise pastors and lay leaders who serve in smaller churches recognize that they do not have to be isolated from the larger body of gifts and graces that Christ provides for all of his church. We are not sent to build our own little kingdoms, but to joyfully celebrate and utilize all the gifts the Lord has given us through others, and "grow up in every way into him who is the head, into Christ, from whom the whole body, joined and knit together by every ligament with which it is equipped, as each part is working properly, promotes the body's growth in building itself up in love" (Eph. 4:15-16).

4. Sunday Worship and Preaching

Leander Keck, writes:

Renewing any institution requires revitalizing its core, its reason for being. Unless this core is refocused and funded afresh, renewal becomes a matter of strategy for survival. Accordingly, the churches' renewal becomes possible only when their religious vitality is energized again by a basic reform of their worship of God.[6]

The renewal of churches is not the same as secular endeavors when hunting about for a strategy. Rather it is what happens when the people of God "repent," when they "turn away" from all their other forms and fashions, and stand before Almighty God with mouths and souls full of praise to the One who is worthy. Worship is not a strategic means to some other end, it is the end itself, the goal of our living and dying. And, Keck adds, "in the praiseful worship of God, the role of preaching is vital. In fact, renewal, preaching, and praise belong together."[7]

Almost every book published on ministry in the smaller church has at least one chapter on worship or preaching. Several years ago

Will Willimon and Bob Wilson worked together to produce *Preaching and Worship in the Small Church*.[8] More recently, Laurence Wagley has contributed a text on what he calls "participatory biblical narrative preaching."[9] In many smaller churches, preaching and worship are all there is.

The pastors in our study confirm this priority. When asked what their congregations do best, they respond: (1) love and accept others, (2) prepare wonderful meals, and (3) worship the Lord. When asked what factors have contributed most to the growth they have experienced, they mention: (1) love and acceptance, (2) pastoral initiative, (3) new programs and ministries, and (4) alive, open worship. When asked, however, what they do best, they rank their roles as preachers (1) and teachers (5) much higher than their work as worship leaders (16). Yet they perceive that the various elements of worship such as prayer, music, celebration, openness to God, love for one another, and preaching God's Word all work together to make the Sunday morning service the most important single cause of renewal and turnaround in their churches. More than in any other way, it is in worship that smaller congregations turn to the Spirit and find new life.

David Lattimer, a scholar-leader in a small denomination in the Midwest, undertook extensive research to determine which churches were most effective in reaching new persons for Christ. As part of his research he visited ten churches as a participant observer. Five churches (Group A) had the highest number of professions of faith the previous year. The other five (Group B) had none. Reporting on preaching in these churches he writes:

> I experienced the preaching as excellent in two of the group A churches and good in the other three. Two of the sermons were 15 minutes or less in length, while the other three averaged about 30 minutes. In group B one sermon was good, while three others were weak. Of the three weak sermons, one was very negative, in another the pastor read a sermon from a periodical, and in the third the pastor apologized for his sermon. In the fifth church of group B the pastor refused to preach and insisted that I do it.[10]

Excellent preaching makes a critical difference. And more and more turnaround preachers in small churches are leaving their notes and manuscripts behind, moving away from their pulpits, and learning to communicate biblical truths through the intimate media of stories and modern parables.

One young pastor and preacher, Richard Thornton, credits to this frightening and yet empowering style of preaching much of the sense of renewal both he and the congregation are now experiencing. When he was first contacted by a denominational leader and asked to consider moving from the staff of a church in Ohio to pastor a struggling Church of God in the tiny crossroads community of Yocumtown, Pennsylvania, he responded "I'm not much of a preacher." But he learned. He says "In seminary I was taught to preach from a manuscript. That's all I knew. I tried it for eight years. But four years ago I shifted to using only notes, and then to stories and no notes. It has radically changed my experience and effectiveness as a preacher."

To prepare for preaching he reads the lectionary and the works of contemporary Christian poets and storytellers. The goal is to create totally thematic worship and preach the biblical message focusing on one point, leaving the people with the sense that they have had their minds and eyes opened to God. A worship team of about six persons meets together weekly to plan and pray. Music has become more and more focused on helping the congregation join together in praising God. Drama is used once a month. This congregation was not much more than a skeleton when Rich arrived. But he accepted the call anyway, and he stayed. In 1994 they are in a new $500,000 worship center seating over two hundred, and two worship services are offered every Sunday morning.

In worship, *personal* and *corporate renewal* happens. Here, under the inspired and anointed preaching of biblical yet contemporary messages, *conceptual* and *missiological renewal* is set in motion as a new vision of being God's people and doing God's work is taught and caught. It is from this kind of worship—alive, open, prayerful, Bible-centered, expectant, participatory, joyful, God-focused—that the flame is rekindled.

5. Small Groups

It has been argued by some that the small church *is* a small group; it doesn't *have* small groups. In reality, however, anytime a small church has a group that gathers other than for worship, it is supporting some form of small group emphasis. Something happens when three, six, or ten people gather to talk and pray and read from the Bible.

Although there are many reasons people join together in small groups (Twelve Step programs, age-level fellowships, sharing and prayer groups, ministry teams, recreational teams, and so on), the most common is Bible study.[11] For some it is the standard "Wednesday Night Bible Study." Others offer special short-term opportunities like the Serendipity materials of Lyman Coleman. Many in United Methodist churches are engaged in the new Disciple Bible studies. Like Bethel Bible, Trinity, and other long-term Bible study programs, these groups require a serious commitment to read and reflect on the Word. In the course of almost a year together, those who engage in this type of focused fellowship find themselves deeply renewed in their love for one another and for the divine vision given through the pages of Scripture.

James Cushman created a model to bring *conceptual* and *missiological renewal* to the Beverly Presbyterian Church in West Virginia. He writes: "The pastor is a teacher, . . . but a pastor cannot force and direct this process of growth in people. This must be a natural process that occurs as people in a congregation learn how to study the Bible and theology together and reflect upon their own life situation."[12] After serving as their pastor for four years, he began a year-long program aimed at congregational recommitment. In the spring he selected a task force of four persons to work with him over the next nine months on the design and a trial run of the proposed six-week small group study process.

In January of the following year members of the task force became leaders of four small groups. The congregation and inactive members were all invited to participate in six weeks of exploring the Bible, reviewing the meaning of church membership from The Book of Church Order, evaluating the meaning of having a personal belief system, and considering the practical implications of such a faith. Following the meetings, each group outlined their own composite statement of what it meant to be a church member. After a church-wide dinner in March where each of the groups reported, a writing team was selected to compose the new statement of membership commitment to be used on Easter Sunday.

55

Cushman writes:

One result of the study program was an immediate increase in the level of commitment, interest, and participation on the part of a number of persons in the church. . . .

Any small church that is involved in a process of revitalization needs to be engaged in study in order to discover new directions and new identity. As that new direction and identity emerges, the congregation is then ready to begin planning how it can achieve its mission.[13]

Like the early church, whose members gave themselves to "the apostles' teaching and fellowship" (Acts 2:42), congregations are being turned around today because disciples are committing themselves to the same disciplines as they meet together both in "the temple" and "from house to house."

6. Community Involvement

Normally the progression of new life in turnaround churches is from some combination of *personal* and *corporate renewal* to *conceptual* and *structural renewal*, and finally to *missiological renewal*. But a growing number of both individuals and congregations are finding the key to turnaround begins with mission to others.

In a society increasingly composed of aging baby boomers and their offspring, discovering a meaningful mission to invest one's life in is often truly a life-changing experience. More and more "older second career persons" are entering seminary in preparation for some form of full-time Christian ministry. Why? For some it is because of a wonderful new personal and corporate experience of spiritual renewal through their local church or a program like The Walk to Emmaus. Others find their renewal begins through a short-term experience with Volunteers in Mission, or Habitat for Humanity or helping with the local effort to address the needs of the homeless. They are tired of "playing church." They want to feel that they have given something of themselves to others in need. They seek, in Erik Erikson's terminology, the experiences of generativity and life integrity. It is more blessed to give than to receive. Many baby boomers are at the point in life where they *need* to give, not to get.

Typical of this pattern is this comment from Don Graham, pastor of St. Peter's by the Sea United Methodist Church in Corpus Christi, Texas.

Working with people in the poverty of villages in Mexico taught us dramatically the meaning of loving our brothers. . . . It was almost with a feeling of reluctance that the team picked up and left on Saturday morning. We had become very close to one another, and we had functioned well and accomplished much as a team. We had spent a week together doing hot, dirty, and hard work. Most of us had only one shower all week long. We ate very simple food. But yet, we enjoyed one another's company.

We had a feeling of accomplishment and satisfaction of a job well done. We knew that there was no way that we could satisfy all of the needs; however, we at least had done something. We had done more than just write a check. We had put the rubber to the road in the name of Jesus Christ.

In this experience we learned that what is most important in life is not what we want to do. The most important thing in life is what God wants us to do, and that is to serve other people in the name of Jesus Christ.[14]

St. Peter's by the Sea is a renewed and active church. Its members distribute over 250 food baskets at Christmas. They have developed an innovative and cooperative network of support for persons seeking to recover from drug and alcohol addiction. They provide food, counsel, and support groups for people who are in need. The pastor and the members are experiencing the Holy Spirit's power in many areas, but they are learning above all that turning to the Spirit means doing what the Spirit says. *Missiological renewal* causes many to raise questions about the meaning of their faith and the power of the gospel. *Personal* and *corporate renewal* can follow; and frequently, *conceptual* and *structural renewal* are very close behind. The order is not what is most important. The fact that all areas or dimensions of renewal are in place makes the lasting difference.

Turning Points and Curves

Some smaller churches involved in turnaround can remember absolute turning points when spiritual life rushed in to change almost everything from that day on. These are largely the exceptions, not the rule. Most churches experience spiritual renewal as a curving and mostly unperceived unfolding of grace at work through many channels. It is only later in looking back that they realize all that was happening.

Howard Snyder's five-dimensional model of congregational renewal is a helpful framework to keep in mind as new life in the Spirit is sought and found. Renewal is a total fabric and not merely working hard to design a mission statement, or change the organizational structure, or have individuals experience a wonderful weekend. But nothing is more at the heart of ongoing spiritual refreshment than what happens Sunday after Sunday during worship. Other ingredients may contribute to rekindling the flame in a small church, and several have been mentioned. But a pastor who loves to praise God and joyfully preach the good news, who expectantly prays for the Spirit to come and heal the broken and reclaim the lost, and who unashamedly loves God and the sheep of God's pasture, will be an instrument the Lord will use to restore a vital hope and a bright future to almost any local church.

It is a great calling. It is a great gospel. It is a great hope. And so with our brother Paul, let us pray for ourselves and all the churches of God:

> For this reason I bow my knees before the Father, from whom every family in heaven and on earth takes its name. I pray that, according to the riches of his glory, he may grant that you may be strengthened in your inner being with power through his Spirit, and that Christ may dwell in your hearts through faith, as you are being rooted and grounded in love. I pray that you may have the power to comprehend, with all the saints, what is the breadth and length and height and depth, and to know the love of Christ that surpasses knowledge, so that you may be filled with all the fullness of God. (Eph. 3:14-19)

IV

SIDESTEPPING THE OBSTACLES

Rev. Moore persisted; nearly the entire choir and its director quit. . . . A number of families left the church.[1]

At the end of forty days they returned from spying out the land. And they came to Moses and Aaron and to all the congregation . . . and showed them the fruit of the land. And they told him, "We came to the land to which you sent us; it flows with milk and honey, and this is its fruit. Yet the people who live in the land are strong. . . . and to ourselves we seemed like grasshoppers."

Numbers 13:25, 27, 28, 33

The people of God through every age have been confronted by "giants" of various names, which drive many into fearful retreat, divide God's people against themselves, and create the feeling for almost everyone that they are little more than grasshoppers. When the armies of King Saul were immobilized in battle because they feared the Philistines and their giant warrior Goliath, it took the unconventional approach and the courageous faith of a lad named David to free the Israelites from their bondage. David was absolutely confident of one thing: "the battle is the LORD's and he will give you into our hand" (1 Sam. 17:47). When the spies sent out by Moses returned from the land of Canaan there was a majority report and a minority report. Those frightened that they could not succeed in crossing into the promised land cried out against their leaders, and "said to one another, 'Let us choose a captain, and go back to Egypt'" (Num. 14:4).

John Bunyan's classic tale *Pilgrim's Progress* reminds us that following the guidance of "Evangelist" to "yonder shining light" and the narrow gate of salvation is dangerous and costly. "Christian" discovers that staying on the rough and narrow way is difficult—at times, almost impossible. But Christian Pilgrim knows this is what he must do to obtain his salvation. And although he encounters many distractions, false friends, and deadly beasts, he also is led each step of the way by true friends sent from God who know how to sidestep the obstacles and lead him to the Celestial City. This is the kind of friendship, guidance, and encouragement needed today in smaller churches across this land. This chapter listens as "true friends" guide us around dangerous obstacles and on to the prize of our upward call.

Identifying the Obstacles

Although all the obstacles faced by smaller churches are too many to mention, some problems seem to show up repeatedly. Turnaround pastors who have successfully sidestepped many such snares along the path list their top ten as:

Obstacles Facing Turnaround Leaders

1. A lack of vision for doing God's will
2. A defeatist attitude draining energy from people
3. Members attached to old ways and ideas
4. Inadequate finances
5. Inflexible older members
6. Inadequate or rundown facilities
7. Low levels of faith and commitment

8. A cold shoulder toward outsiders
9. Power cliques that create conflict
10. A survival mentality

Although listed separately, it is clear that some of these distracting demons are related. For example, at least three items are related to the attitude and self-image of the congregation (2, 7, 10). Two items focus on the need for a vision of the future rather than dwelling in the past (1 and 3). Two items deal with conflict between members or the pastor and some members (5 and 9). Two items are related to financial issues (4 and 6). And, although all of this could readily present barriers to "outsiders," there is the specific problem of being "cold" and "closed" to them (8).

As a way to double-check the problems faced by small churches, the pastors were also asked "What three primary factors do you think most impede smaller churches from becoming revitalized and engaged in effective ministry and evangelism?" The ten most frequently mentioned are:

Factors Impeding Revitalization

1. Low congregational self-esteem
2. Fear of change and taking risks
3. No vision for the future
4. An "us versus them" attitude
5. Power cliques in the church
6. Lack of finances and/or stewardship
7. Apathy and burnout
8. Pastors who don't lead
9. Closed to "outsiders"
10. Unwilling to work hard

With the exception of the order they are listed in, and item number eight, the two lists look almost identical.

Thus we can identify five major problems faced by churches and their pastors as they seek to move from a survival mentality to renewed investment in ministry and evangelism. The problems are: (1) low self-esteem and apathy, (2) lack of vision for the future, (3) lack of concern and love for "outsiders," (4) finances and stewardship of resources, and (5) issues of power and interpersonal conflict.

Various forms of these five "dragons of defeat" may raise their ugly heads along the pilgrim path to congregational renewal, and the sequence of their appearance may vary. But let there be no mistake, these are the demons in our day that need to be confronted by any pastor seeking "to proclaim release to the captives and recovery of sight to the blind, to let the oppressed go free, to proclaim the year of the Lord's favor" (Luke 4:18, 19).

Staying on the Path

Mercifully, pastors do not always need to fight all these dragons at once, and they do not have to fight them by themselves. In fact, on occasion the pastors report that they are the beneficiaries of the work of others who went before them. Norma Walters Wingo, a pastor in Durham, North Carolina writes: "When the previous pastor came here five years ago there were six people in Sunday school and about twenty-two in worship. When he moved three years later, attendance had grown to about fifteen in Sunday school and thirty-five in worship. Now the attendance is about forty-five and the church continues to reach out."

Eugene Feagin serves a United Methodist church in South Carolina and describes how each of four pastors contributed to the congregational momentum that led to their turnaround. Ten years before he arrived, a colleague had "pushed" the congregation toward change. His lack of patience, however, created more tension than could be tolerated, and he was asked to leave. A second pastor came to "heal the wounds."

> He worked diligently to draw the people together. He helped them celebrate the ministries they had and led them to see how they might expand their ministries into other areas. He also helped them feel connected to the rest of the denomination in a way they had not before. During this time they were able to sell the old, inadequate "Mill House" (literally part of the old cotton mill) which had served as the parsonage for many years, and purchase a new parsonage close to the homes of many of the members. The youth program became seen as a way to reach out to the community, and a new van was purchased to be used both for the youth and the senior adult group.

An emergency situation elsewhere led to a new appointment for this pastor and a retired interim pastor came for ten months.

He agreed to visit the sick and shut-ins, and the congregation agreed to divide up responsibilities for worship leadership. Each group took turns—the youth, the women, the men, and the seniors. All that this meant to the congregation is yet to be explored, but I am sure this was when a new sense of accomplishment, unity and confidence developed.

It was after the ten months of the interim pastor's ministry that Rev. Feagin arrived. He writes:

In the fifteen months since my family has arrived we have begun building on the work of the former pastors. I have a strong sense that we need to develop a vision statement as a congregation. We have spent a great deal of time in meetings discussing who we are and where we need to go. A special new planning committee has been appointed and is working hard to study our building use and building needs. At present we are planning to build a larger Fellowship building where the church and the community can gather and share in shaping our future. I believe my job is to help our congregation discover their own hidden dreams and find the means to fulfill them as the people of God.

Few pastors work in isolation from the whole history of a congregation. There are those who have gone before and there will be others who follow. Although it can be painful and discouraging to watch progress made during one tenure of leadership experience a setback following a pastoral change, the words of Paul are as critically important for us today as when they were written to the Corinthians in the first century.

What then is Apollos? What is Paul? Servants through whom you came to believe, as the Lord assigned to each. I planted, Apollos watered, but God gave the growth. So neither the one who plants nor the one who waters is anything, but only God who gives the growth. The one who plants and the one who waters have a common purpose, and each will receive wages according to the labor of each. For we are God's servants, working together; you are God's field, God's building. (1 Cor. 3:5-9)

63

In other words, we may not always play exactly the same role for every congregation. Thus, what "worked" last time, may only frustrate things this time. If the planting has already taken place, only watering and weeding is needed. To blindly start at the same place in each new pastorate is the height of arrogance and insensitivity to the Spirit of God.

But when the church has had a major disruption, it is well to note how the "together" language and actions described by Duane Lewellen can show the way to lead a church to health and wholeness.

> The church had a major split a year before I arrived. Together we decided that this congregation needed to work at unity, forgiveness, and change. We decided each step together and openly. A newspaper was started so that every member would be aware of all that was happening and of future plans. I have had no major problems in six years.

What would it look like to start from scratch following the list of major obstacles and impediments to renewal listed by the pastors in our study? It would require first of all that there be a healing of the past and a movement toward healthy congregational unity, otherwise known as "faith, hope, and love."

1. Recovering a Sense of Grace

In much of the literature "self-esteem" is listed as the most critical problem faced by smaller churches. Lyle Schaller writes:

> While it is seldom mentioned, a very significant factor behind the lack of numerical growth in many small congregations (especially among those urban churches that today are only a fraction of the size they were back in the 1950s or 1960s) is the low level of corporate self-esteem among the members. Frequently the members of these congregations see themselves as small, weak, unattractive, powerless, and frustrated with a limited future. That self-image often creates a self-perpetuating cycle that produces policies and decision that inhibit the potential outreach. Their priorities are survival and institutional maintenance, not evangelism.[2]

Many things contribute to this problem: insensitive and untrained leaders, community and demographic changes, conflict between members and/or families in the congregation, inadequate income, aging buildings, loss of members, and rapid turnover of pastors, to name just a few. Small churches, where relationships are most important, quite naturally experience insecurity, doubt, and even anger because of this turnover. One pastor writes "I was the fifth pastor in five years. I had to persuade and show them my willingness to stay and to love and to serve the church."

What is needed to enable a congregation to escape this pit of self-pity? The answer is a renewed sense of the grace of God. But a word of caution. No one ought to try to pull another out of quicksand while standing in it. Pastors anxious to throw a rope of rescue need to make very sure they are secure themselves. Whether young or old, whether experienced or inexperienced in pastoral ministry, the most important quality is one's own inner sense of faith, confidence, and self-worth. It is easy to get dragged in and dragged under. Some become frightened when they are not immediately successful, and they flee—perhaps wisely so. There is no need for anymore casualties than absolutely necessary. Success cannot be defined by any one effort. Sometimes we "fail" if our goal is to always be just the right person for the job, or if we look through short-term spectacles. Paul and Silas were not a big hit in Philippi when they first sought to bring the gospel there (Acts 16), but eventually the church at Philippi blossomed so that Paul could say "I thank my God every time I remember you, . . . confident of this, that the one who began a good work among you will bring it to completion" (Phil. 1:3, 6).

Thomas Albert, looking back on successfully helping a church to regain its vision and grow during his first seven years of ministry as a second career pastor, writes:

> Ministers going through this must expect some hurt and pain. This kind of growth can be scary and threatening. The minister can become the whipping post. It is not personal, but it hurts just the same. Often I thought of moving; however, I needed to stay, become part of their hurt, and facilitate the growth. In two or three years this church will be over the hump; and I would be remiss not to add, the praise and glory for all this belongs to God.

Steve Porter counsels:

Expect little or no real support from the church at first, rather expect skepticism, cynicism, and no desire for growth. Therefore, expect to do a lot of early work on your own. Be prepared for the unexpected, perhaps a volunteer will show up to help visit. Each church will be different as to the type of evangelism that will work; a revival at one, knocking on doors at another. Be prepared to be innovative, as in making room for more Sunday school classes when there is no room. Don't be disappointed if there are no results right away; and don't compare your "accomplishments" with other pastors.

Once the "reality check" on a pastor's ego and expectations has been run, what practical steps can be taken to help a negatively charged or passively resigned congregation regain a solid footing in God's grace and be energized for their future?

First, turnaround pastors counsel: "control what you can, not what you can't." Learn to lead from personal strengths with a positive approach. Don't attack the resistance, but announce and demonstrate a grace-filled gospel. Be convinced of God's call to your particular congregation, and share their sense of "honor" in being placed there by God for the wonderful things that are to happen.

Second, to help create a sense of openness, they suggest "Be open." Dennis Rinehart from Warren, Ohio writes: "Set the pace by being open yourself, and open your parsonage to your people. Have them share how they came to faith and/or to this church, what they like, and what they would like to change. Begin where your people are."

Third, visit everyone, listen, and when appropriate, share your own faith story and dreams for the church. Meet with any group that will have you. Look for opportunities to meet with a men's breakfast group (formal or informal), a women's circle, the youth—even if there isn't an official youth fellowship. Take them for an outing.

Fourth, make sure you serve as pastor working from a theological and faith base, not merely as the manager of an institution. One pastor commented: "Without the grace of God, humankind is on a course of self-destruction at all levels. God has called me to help people discover their sacred self-worth in Him that they will never see apart from Christ. I believe that God wants people to be whole again, healed from the brokenness of sin." See the people as Jesus did and have compassion on them as Christ's shepherd (Matt. 9:35-38).

Fifth, learn to respect, affirm, encourage, and compliment every-one you can for anything you can. Bob Chapman from Arcadia, Florida writes:

> The respect of a congregation is the first step in restoration. Our idea of who they are, becomes to them, the hope and pattern of what they may become. Congregational elevation to self-respect requires a great deal of work on the individuals within the congregation. Respect the refuse collector as much as the banker and vice versa. Jesus did this, and he taught it to Peter and the other disciples. To restore a church from lostness to effectiveness, we must work on the individual's and the congregation's self-respect at the same time. We must learn the art of giving sincere, honest praise. Do not condemn, criticize or complain. Show them a better way.

This is not just an approach to interpersonal relationships. Share with others in the congregation the good things that are going on. Post achievements, birthdays, anniversaries, news items, and thank-you notes on the bulletin board. Tell the old-timers who have given their best to the church for decades that you know how much they have done.

Sixth, whenever appropriate and possible, attract recognition from outside. Get a newspaper writer to cover some special event or write the article yourself and submit it. Include a photograph when-ever possible. A picture is still worth a thousand words, or more. Invite denominational officials to come visit without an agenda except to enjoy worship and thank God for this congregation.

Seventh, involve the congregation in worship, and preach mes-sages designed to reveal the grace of God at work today. Earlier we noted that worship is the centerpiece of spiritual renewal. But wor-ship truly needs to be the work and joy of all God's people. Invite members of all ages to participate. Make it the whole family sharing together in the presence of God. Ask one to share a testimony, another to sing a song, or lead the prayer, or read the scripture, or bake the bread and help serve communion. And when it is time for the message, Willis Osban from Manila, Arkansas catches the spirit of grace-full preaching when he writes: "I used stories from the Bible about people being used of God even when they were small and powerless in the face of difficulty. I emphasized the truth of being new persons in Christ. We are important. I had them try one thing at a time. Their confidence grew as they experienced success."

Eighth, help them experience success and celebrate a victory. Richard Paul suggests: "Love them and lead them. Give them what they need—change—not what they want. How? Don't give up. Start and complete small programs to emphasize progressiveness. Applaud areas of change and growth and then challenge the next step in the process." Patty Beagle was appointed as a part-time local (meaning, not ordained) pastor to a dying church with an average attendance of five. She writes from West Virginia:

> We had a workday at the church and twenty-five people came. We got a lot done and surprised ourselves. Then we finished a project that had been hanging in the balance for five years (a new outhouse and a parking lot). I rang the church bells for the first time in ten years.

This is a church learning to celebrate the grace of God and catch a vision for new life.

2. Imparting a New Vision

When turnaround pastors are asked how they sidestep the obstacles, by far their number one answer is to teach and preach a new vision for serving God. The goal of becoming a turnaround church is not merely more money, more activity, more members, and more goodwill. These might all be signs that something good is happening, but there is a need for every congregation to clearly recognize its identity as the church of Jesus Christ planted by God for the benefit of all who can be reached by its ministry and message of salvation.

According to the J. B. Phillips translation of the New Testament, the First Letter of Paul to the Thessalonians begins:

> To the church of the Thessalonians, founded on God the Father and the Lord Jesus Christ, grace and peace from Paul, Silvanus and Timothy.
>
> We are always thankful to God as we pray for you all, for we never forget that your faith has meant solid achievement, your love has meant hard work, and the hope that you have in our Lord Jesus Christ

means sheer dogged endurance in the life that you live before God, the Father of us all.

We know, brothers, that God not only loves you but has selected you for a special purpose. For we remember how our gospel came to you not as mere words, but as a message with power behind it—the convincing power of the Holy Spirit. . . . You have become a sort of sounding-board from which the Word of the Lord has rung out. (1 Thess. 1:1-5, 8 JBP)

What a difference might it make for members of a congregation to spend time reading these verses and then ask themselves: "What is our church founded on?" "What does that mean?" "How much prayer is being invested for our church?" "What has our faith, hope, and love meant?" "Do we know God loves us?" "What is our special purpose?" "Can we remember how the gospel first came to us?" "How do others see the effectual power of the Holy Spirit in us?" "How does the Word of the Lord ring out from us?"

Helping to impart a congregational vision is not the same as working out a strategic plan or writing a mission statement. It is more a matter of "seeing" things the way they are intended to be, and can be, and will be, by God's grace. What can a pastor do to help clarify and empower this vision?

First, pastors who lead congregations to find a corporate vision, have a personal vision already at work in their own lives. They believe in a personal God who intervenes in history and changes people. Their own experiences of conversion or their call to ministry are vivid, and they are thus convinced that God is ready and able to touch the lives of others. Greg Crispell from Waterport, New York says "The Holy Spirit is God's gift for the church. Jesus and the healing touch of Jesus in my life brings a constant confirmation of the power of this reality in the face of every challenge." Hal Nobel from Anniston, Alabama writes:

I was truly lost in the world of living for money and material things when I realized I was sad and lonely within myself. I had tried everything else to discover satisfaction, but only when I said yes to God did I begin to experience the real substance of life. It has given me a sense of joy knowing that there is real hope for all persons in finding Christ as Lord of all.

69

Second, preach and teach the redemptive and loving activity of God and the purpose of God for the church. Avoid moralisms and lessons on the oughts. Focus first on what God does before emphasizing our response. David Bromstad puts it this way: "Develop a vision based on God's ability not human ability. The best days of the church you serve are always ahead, not behind. Immerse yourself in God's word and pray seeking Him. Wait on His response, then go with it. The results are His concern." Along the same lines Kirk Morledge writes from Wisconsin:

> We try to help people see themselves and their church's mission in the pages of the Scriptures. For example, the day we bought our new site, we erected "12 stones" in the worship service (Josh. 4). The day we dedicated the new site with a worship service outside on the site, we celebrated the completion of our journey to "The Promised Land," and allowed everyone there to sign a "Pilgrim Roll." Help your people find themselves and their church in the Bible. They are there.

Third, "re-member" and celebrate the heritage of the church. Every church, except a new congregation, has a history. The Holy Spirit has been active in the lives and events of the past. Carl Dudley dedicates a chapter to this activity of remembering in his book *Making the Small Church Effective*.[3] Many churches recover a sense of their heritage and identity by telling the old stories in new ways (a drama, a written history, a heritage quilt, stories about the memorial gifts, a special series of "Heritage Days," old fashioned testimonies of "I remember when God . . ."). For his D.Min. project, Joseph DiPaolo used testimony, letters, narrative, and photographs to compose the story of faith of the church he was then serving. Then he published it. In the preface he writes:

> I hope you will both enjoy and be encouraged by what follows, and be able to discern within its pages the gracious leading of God, who has been calling, testing, refining, and transforming lives after the image of Christ in and through a particular community of people now known as Wissinoming United Methodist Church.[4]

To remember what God has done among us in the past, even though we were not perfect, can encourage people to dream dreams and see visions for the future.

70

Fourth, provide intentional and structured opportunities for members to voice their dreams and visions, perhaps a day apart with leaders or during a series of Sunday evenings. David Bromstad writes: "We have a day apart for planning and fellowship. It helps them see the whole picture. Two members asked me 'What do you mean the best days are in front of us?' We shared with them our vision. They picked up the vision and began to get excited about their potential."

Fifth, ask good questions. Ed Kerr reports from Arkansas, "I surveyed the congregation with questions that would cause them to think." An example of such questions and a way to ask them is modeled above with the J. B. Phillips translation of 1 Thessalonians 1. Other questions recommended include: "Whose church is this?" "Why are you here?" "What business are we in?"

Sixth, work together to arrive at a common vision of what God is calling the congregation to be and to do. The answer might come out as simple as one sentence, or a phrase such as "Making room for our neighbors in the fellowship of faith" or "A warm church that shows the love of God and ministers to all people in a fresh New Testament atmosphere." Or, it may be more like what Dennis Hamshire reports as the dream statement of the Green Street Church of God in Harrisburg, Pennsylvania, which reads:

> To be the center or focal point of our community and to see our Church filled with people. To get more young people involved to carry forth our religious beliefs. To attractively maintain and utilize our existing facility to its maximum potential and to expand as we grow in response to meeting needs.

Seventh, as the congregational vision becomes clearer, begin to establish priorities for investing your own gifts and energy in light of congregational expectations and the vision. William Keeffe, a former conference council director and district superintendent and now a pastor serving a smaller church in Bow, New Hampshire writes:

> The "Setting of Priorities for Pastoral Ministry" exercise made me aware of how I as a pastor have assumed people in my parish know my concepts of ministry and are aware of my efforts to carry these

71

out in day to day activities. It seems there is inadequate communication between pastor and people relating to what we do on the "other six days of the week." This is not to say we need to punch a time clock or fill out "monthly reports" including each day's activities, but we do need to share what we do with our people and let them know how we vision our ministry.

His own list goes something like this: (1) people, (2) preaching, (3) worship services, (4) visitation, (5) unchurched families, (6) small groups, (7) pastoral counseling, (8) new leaders, (9) saying no, (10) "In times of change, rearrange!" As a pastor more clearly establishes his or her priorities in line with personal giftedness, God's call, and the congregational vision, others will recognize that "adjusting" is what all of us do as we follow the leading of the Holy Spirit into a new and brighter future and reach out to others offering Christ.

3. Extending Concern to Outsiders

Anytime a family is facing its own internal struggles with damaged relationships, guilt, feelings of betrayal, loss of income, death of a family member, or stress from any number of causes, the tendency is to pull in on itself. Fewer friends are invited over. Every new challenge, even the small ones, feels like a burden too heavy to carry. Depression sets in. Conflict is always just below the surface, or exploding out into the open. As time passes, some healing may take place. But unless real forgiveness and redemption are experienced, it is not likely that this is going to be an ideal home for foster children, or the best place for a son or daughter to live after a divorce, or a haven for a widowed mother-in-law to find love and comfort.

Healthy families are wonderful gifts of God because they offer the energy of faith, hope, and love to one another and to many outsiders who just "happen by." The love and respect spill over into the world around and invite response like the wagging tail of a small puppy. Families in the midst of blaming one another or when under enormous stress do not seem to offer the same welcome. They are like wounded insects curling inward on themselves. People may notice, but most won't want to stay and watch. A small church is like family. When it is emotionally and spiritually healthy, it is very attractive. When it is turned inward in anger and pain, or self-preoccupation, it is not.

How can pastors and church leaders help small churches turn their survival-focused fears into excitement about reaching out to others?

In the first place, turning toward the Spirit, recovering of grace, and imparting a new vision need to be underway. It could be said that once love and the power of the Spirit are moving again to heal those who have waited a long time for hope, the natural direction for the flow of energy and love is outward toward friends and family. This is not a simple "one, two, three" approach, since even though new people are seen as desirable to help carry the load, there is also the fear that they will take control and change things. But, as Gerald Shoap from Hanover, Pennsylvania sums it up: "They first need to know their own needs are cared for, then they can learn the other truth of the gospel—'love your neighbor.'"

Second, the pastor cannot just announce that outreach is important or a command of God. She or he needs to lead the way. As a new sense of joyful worship and warmth are being rekindled, the pastor needs to engage in personal outreach and evangelism, most naturally to those who constitute the "extended family" of the members.

Shortly after arriving at my own appointment to a smaller church in Arizona, one of the women in the congregation asked if I would call on her husband who never attended. He had the reputation of being a "strange duck." He loved the desert and worked with the Scout program, but didn't have much use for preachers and church. I dropped by one Saturday afternoon. No one answered the door. I left a card saying, "Sorry I missed you." Later that evening as I was putting some finishing touches on my sermon, the phone rang. The man's voice on the other end simply said, "Are you really?" I was confused by his inquiry, and repeated my name asking if he had the right number. He responded, "Are you *really* sorry?" and then added, "that you missed me." Aha, the weight of the words finally clicked. I hesitatingly replied "Yes, . . . I think so." He asked, "When are you coming by next? I'll be here." I grew to love Ben as one of my dearest friends, and he grew to love the Lord and the church. Pastors who visit, reach out, and invite open the door outward and lead the way for the congregation to follow.

Third, stimulate the imagination of individuals and the entire congregation by asking good questions about outreach such as: "When was the last time you invited someone to church? Who are the people around us here who are not involved in a church? Why do you suppose they don't attend? What difference would it make in our community if this church were overflowing with people week after week? What are the problems in the community that need to be addressed? Could we do something about them?"

Fourth, share the stories of other churches that have struggled back from defeat to new life and hope and effective ministry and growth. If this is done too soon, it only frustrates people with a feeling that they are being compared to others; they will think that they are failures or less valuable than those "other" churches that happened to have different situations and weren't facing the same kinds of problems. But when enough stories can be shared at the right time, with the right people, it stimulates ideas about what could happen here.

Fifth, a little success in seeing new faces and the return of old familiar faces long absent goes a long way to change the attitude of evangelistic outreach. Likewise, the sense of having made a real difference in the lives of others through a caring ministry reminds everyone that serving in love is its own blessing. Captain Roger Windell, serving the Salvation Army congregation in Grand Forks, North Dakota, says: "As new people began coming, our people lowered their defenses, and their attitude changed to one of acceptance. This generated a new excitement within the congregation. Suddenly the members became proud and jumped on the bandwagon."

Sixth, the best energy and concern for outreach simply comes because people recognize themselves as blessed. In God's divine providence, when the Spirit of God has wrought "a new creation" and "everything has become new" (2 Cor. 5:17), the people of God are led as was Paul to discover they are "ambassadors for Christ" (5:20). One view of this picture of being reconciled and discovering the ministry of reconciliation was contributed by Marcelle Myers, who, as a second career pastor, has served Nesby Chapel in Nahunta, Georgia, for seven years, a multi-denominational church on a four-point charge.

Members here have established a new commitment to outreach and mission. As pastor here over the last few years, I have seen the church go from being very conservative in the outreach area to being very

74

liberal. They were contented, or maybe complacent is a better word, with things as they were. At the beginning of my tenure here, we set some specific goals to expand our facilities. This activity and involvement seemed to lift the passivity from this congregation and when this project was completed, new ideas came forth on the best way to use these facilities in meeting the needs of the local community. New committees were formed and more outreach ministries were started. The passive stance of the congregation was changed into an active one and a sense of progress surfaced and we all celebrated a victory.

4. Expanding the Financial Base

In the Nesby Chapel revitalization described above, the church began to discover how to reach out after their own facilities were upgraded and expanded. Some writers and prophetic voices today are opposed to spending any more money on buildings. This isn't a new idea. The hermits of ancient days decided the best way to find spiritual renewal was to abandon all claim to any material attachments and live in the simplest of conditions. This ascetic lifestyle was seen as more faithful to Jesus who himself had "nowhere to lay his head" (Matt. 8:20) and who seemed to speak against building larger barns to store the harvest (Luke 12:13-21). But these naysayers and misinterpreters of the texts neglect to notice that Jesus accepted invitations to even the nicest of homes, regularly attended synagogue and visited the temple for worship, and counseled against storing up treasures for ourselves, but not against spending money—especially for the business of the kingdom: "For where your treasure is, there your heart will be also" (Luke 12:34).

Pastors of small churches frequently report "inadequate finances and poor stewardship are a constant problem, and the facilities are poorly maintained and inadequate." Therefore, one of the most practical and important problems tackled by successful pastors is to find and free the money needed to upgrade the church facilities and instill a new sense of pride and power. There may be no easier way initially to enlist both finances and effort, especially from men in the congregation, than through a program to enhance the structures owned by the church. If the vision of what is possible has begun to be instilled in the people and the first signs of new life and new members have been recognized, it is time to invest in the future. Six strategies to leap the "finances and facilities" obstacle emerge from the experiences of our turnaround pastors.

First, don't make the mistake of assuming that there is no money, either already available but hidden, or potentially in the families supporting the church. Several stories were told concerning discovering major funds unknown to most members of the church. Treasurers and other financial officers who have served the church over many years are frequently quite conservative about spending money, and may have a strong sense of being the guardians of church funds against the "unnecessary" projects recommended by the parade of new pastors or "those denominational people." Their interest in protecting the church's monies may, in time, become its own special form of ownership and control.

One pastor discovered $72,000 in certificates of deposit not on the records and thus hidden from the denomination. Another pastor reported finding—through intentional and resented "snooping" in things that "were none of his business"—$12,000 in an account marked "building fund." At the time he was a college student living with his family in a four-hundred-square-foot converted chicken coop "parsonage" and trying to remind the little church meeting in their old, open-country, white-frame chapel that they needed to provide better if they were ever going to attract a regular pastor. They had been through three pastors in the six months before he naïvely accepted the invitation. He stayed for thirteen years through many dangers, toils, and snares. He finished college and seminary and helped the church become a fully functioning, revitalized congregation. There were eighteen resident members and twelve were in worship the first Sunday he arrived. By last year when he accepted his first new appointment, the church had built one new parsonage and was considering purchasing another, it had purchased land and built a new sanctuary and education facility, it was holding two services and averaging over two hundred, and its annual budget was $150,000. Don't assume there isn't any money. Look for it, and ask for it.

Second, no matter how difficult for the pastor's family to make ends meet on the salary provided, it is critically important to model financial stewardship—even sacrificial giving and tithing—if it is going to be taught or preached to the members. Some pastors avoid the subject entirely and simply say, "I leave that to the lay people."

This is a mistake. Giving is a spiritual discipline and needs to be addressed as such by the spiritual leader.

When the time comes to talk about stewardship for the sake of realizing dreams and recovering a sense of vitality for the future, what leaders do, both clergy and lay—speaks much louder than what they say. In reality, stewardship, like faith, is more caught than taught!

There is no need to tell anyone how much to give, but there is a need to tell why to give and how to make stewardship decisions. When the pastor leads in this matter as a sign of deep commitment to Christ and his church in *this* place, it says "we" are going to make it, and the Lord will provide.

It is discouraging to know that some pastors communicate by announcement or simply by lack of regular and sacrificial giving that they believe their "tithe" is contained in having to work for such small remuneration. No church can be led to true stewardship by one who refuses to practice it. This is itself a form of boycott and anger, neither of which works well to renew a congregation in grace and accomplish the miracles that seem beyond reach. One pastor reported that during his second year the parsonage was broken into, he received death threats, and in other subtle ways was told to "MOVE." He stuck it out because he knew he was called to that church. After the sixth year, he went one morning to get in his twenty-year-old Volkswagen with 200,000 miles on it and found an envelope in the front seat with 160 hundred-dollar bills in it and a short note that read, "new car." Faithful and sacrificial stewardship begets faithful and sacrificial stewardship.

Third, remember that the initial goal is to change the sense of congregational pride or self-esteem. Ed Kerr writes from Plainview, Arkansas:

> Step one was to cause the people to take pride in the appearance of their church building—new sidewalks, wheelchair ramp, fellowship hall renovated, grass neatly mowed and trimmed weekly. Bulletin boards are changed regularly, . . . the church now has the appearance that something is going on here.

There may be more important projects needing to be done, but first work together to give a fresh face to what is already constructed or

77

add that relatively inexpensive change that will say to insiders and outsiders alike, "We're on the move." Anyone who has lived in a home for more than six months no longer sees the tarnish, cracks, and unfinished projects the way visitors do. Our home had a half-painted bathroom door that was almost never noticed or mentioned until we began to think of putting the house up for sale. New people will more likely feel welcomed as visitors if the church buildings and facilities are "attractive." Think about the meaning of that word.

Fourth, focus on financial stewardship as a spiritual discipline and not primarily a way to raise money or pay bills. Small churches, like families, are much more oriented toward paying the bills than they are toward long-range financial planning for the future. To shift from bill paying to planned giving and effective stewardship involves a shift in values, which will come as dreams and visions are linked to spiritual renewal. Money is a gift of God to be invested for the glory of God in accomplishing the things of God.

Larry Frank pastors the Conestoga United Methodist Church in Conestoga, Pennsylvania. This church employs The Walk to Emmaus program as part of their approach to spiritual renewal. He reports that as lives have been spiritually refreshed, and as the church has tried to do something significant in the community, the end-of-the-month financial statement has gone from showing what wasn't paid, to having a regular surplus of $1,200 a month. A woman in the church said boldly:

> One of the most important factors contributing to our growth was we learned how to spend money. Our women's group was reminded by one of our members, "You don't get money if you don't spend money." Before, we never had any money and people were always complaining. Now, because we've decided there are so many things needing to be done, we're raising and spending ten times what we used to and now no one complains.

Fifth, be creative and imaginative in both stewardship education and in raising money. It ought to be fun to give as well as rewarding. Small churches benefit enormously from the fellowship that accompanies special fund raising projects. Patty Beagle describes how their small church in West Virginia learned how to give regularly, but also enjoyed "fund raisers such as the fall bazaar, selling Easter Candy, bake sales and white elephant sales, and special collections for the needy whenever necessary. An 'Outreach Jar' is used each month for a different cause such as the improvement fund, for a family burned out of their home, for two children who were burned, and for hunger."

Sixth, affirm the efforts made and continue to pray for and expect great things, and they will come. Rich Moore pastors the Maple Hill United Methodist Church in Howard City, Michigan. This quote from one of the church's lifelong members, Don Bauman, captures an attitude of stewardship that has become part of the church's identity. "For a small church we carry a pretty heavy financial burden, but we're a six lane church when it comes to giving." For a church to know it is a "six lane" church, and act like a "six lane" church in a "one horse town," requires at least one bold voice to create the momentum and the motto.

Saying "Thank you" for every job well done is especially important in smaller fellowships. There are always subtle dangers connected with our giving. We do it for many reasons, and not all of them are as spiritual as others. But joyful gratitude is an appropriate response to almost every gift offered in Jesus' name and for his work. It usually takes four to six years for complete turnaround to come in most churches. Giving is not only linked to spiritual renewal and vision, but to trust. Trust takes time. But pastors who have learned to say how much they appreciate the efforts of their people are laying a foundation that will stand the times of trial and the test of storms. Persons in any family need to hear that someone is proud of them.

5. Handling Snakes and Other Conflicts

Here in Kentucky it is not unusual to read occasionally about someone in the mountains who was bitten by a poisonous snake during a worship service. In fact, I have provided the opportunity for seminary students to visit these churches as part of their cross-cultural exposure and as an introduction to folk religions. These images came to mind when I heard a pastor in Florida recount the following experience: A woman who had been visiting his church told a friend at work where she had been attending worship. Her friend immediately showed agitation and warned her to not go back to that church because she had heard that it was one of those

79

"snake-handling churches." The woman was surprised but called the pastor to set the record straight. Indeed, as it turned out, a newly hired custodian had spread this story after overhearing a conversation in the sanctuary between the pastor's spouse and a sound system consultant. The consultant clearly did say they would need a "snake" (in audio language, a large bundle of cables all bound together to keep individual wires from each having to be taped down or run separately). The pastor's spouse asked how big a snake it would have to be. The consultant answered, "I can't say for sure, but a big one."

All snakes don't look alike or bite the same way, but when the heat gets turned up in the middle of changes, we ought to be ready for whatever might come out of the fire (Acts 28:3-6). The "snakes" most likely to emerge in times of change when the fires of the Spirit are beginning to blaze are those involving power struggles and interpersonal conflict.

Handling these snakes of conflict, like handling anything dangerous, requires courage, faith, gentleness, and skill. This skill has to do with "gifts and graces" as well as training. Some will "naturally" be better at it than others. But all who hope to be turnaround leaders might as well face the reality that they will have plenty of opportunity to learn by experience if by no other method.

General conflict management theory[5] describes several options for how persons respond to conflict. Norman Shawchuck and Robert Moeller describe these in an article entitled "Animal Instincts: Five ways church members will react in a fight."[6]

> We all develop survival responses in threatening situations. Corporate psychologists have labeled these responses with animal names (for the solutions they seek): sharks ("I win; you lose"), foxes ("Everyone wins a little and loses a little"), turtles ("I withdraw"), teddy bears ("I'll lose so you can win"), and owls ("Let's find a way for everyone to win").

The value of identifying these five "creatures" is not only to show how different members react, but also to recognize and evaluate our own approaches to handling conflict.

Some of us, especially the relational types who like small churches because relationships are highly valued, tend to function like turtles, teddy bears, or foxes. We handle conflict by avoidance, submission, or egalitarian compromise. The first approach will never be a leader for change. Change produces conflict. To avoid conflict is to abdicate leadership. Pastors can function this way and be loved, but they cannot lead a church out of trouble. The second approach sounds most "Christian" to some ears, and passages like "blessed are the peacemakers" (Matt. 5:9) and "Do nothing from selfish ambition or conceit, but in humility regard others as better than yourselves" (the self-emptying *kenosis* passage from Philippians 2:3ff.) come to mind. But teddy bears will always be eaten by sharks. And there is a danger in giving too much away to sharks. Shawchuck and Moeller write: "When 'I must win' individuals are allowed to rule the church, anger builds in others, people feel coerced, and a dangerous dependency on the strong-willed individual develops."[7] This is true whether the shark is a member or a pastor.

The compromise suggested by foxes solves all problems in the same way: "Divide the living boy in two; then give half to the one, and half to the other" (1 Kings 3:25). Solomon's wisdom and the woman who truly loved the child saw through the folly of such a mechanical and egalitarian approach to equality. Such an approach may work well in some situations, but it can also destroy the dynamic and responsive life of the church as Christ's body, which does not exist simply to make everyone happy, but to serve the purposes of the risen Lord.

The recommended approach is that of the collaborative owl. The authors write, "Collaborators see disputes as an opportunity to strengthen a group, not destroy it."[8] They describe three important tasks necessary for wise owls to handle conflict as collaborators ("co-labor"ers). First, generate as much useful information as possible about all sides of the issue. Second, help the group see where they agree not just where they don't. And third, bring all who are involved into the decision-making process and motivate them to personally commit themselves to the final agreement. This is indeed hard work. In fact, it can't always be the approach to every conflict. Sometimes it is best to withdraw. (Does it really matter if the memorial table is in the "right" place?) Sometimes it is necessary to be a shark, or bulldog, and say "Here I stand! I can do nothing else. God help me! Amen."[9] But when it comes time for the church to turn the corner for its future, only the owl can solve the conflict in a way that leads to life and health and peace.

Some issues, and even some persons, need to be confronted head on. Others need to be waited out. Others need to be waded through. Pray for wisdom to know the difference. Be careful, but don't be afraid of the snakes. Sometimes, as the consultant recommended to the church in Florida, a congregation needs a good "snake" to let the new song be heard loud and clear by everyone. Handle the snakes when necessary, but do it, as our Appalachian friends remind us, in the Spirit and in faith. Above all, don't pretend they aren't present or dangerous. But keep loving and keep leading. That is the meaning of God's call to pastoral ministry.

Fresh Fish

John Goering, pastor of the Lewis United Methodist Church in Lewis, Kansas shares this fable:

> I once heard the story of a fisherman who had a secret for preserving fish in the days before refrigeration. Everyone back then kept their fish alive in deep wells in the ships. But his fish were always firm and fresh and better than the others. He consistently got a better market price than his competitors, and they longed to know his secret. After his death his fellow fishermen went on board his ship to search for the secret. They discovered an enormous flathead catfish in the well. Though he ate a few of the fish dumped in, the real benefit of his presence was that he kept all the other fish moving, stirred up, and on the alert. If you will, he kept them "fresh."

Rev. Goering explained the images; but perhaps they are best left, as are most parables, to be discovered. We move next to some reflections on fishing—for people.

V

TURNING TOWARD OTHERS

Do not fear, or be afraid;
have I not told you from of old
and declared it?
You are my witnesses!
Is there any god besides me?
There is no other rock; I know
not one.

Isaiah 44:8

Small-church approaches to evangelism need to be person centered. This is the pattern and strength of the small church. Super churches attract people through their winsome pulpiteer and their glamorous programs. The small church attracts through the contacts people have with its members.[1]

Evangelism—Whose Task?

It would be difficult to read the Bible and not recognize God's desire to seek and to save humanity. This is accomplished through

God's redemptive acts in history, and ultimately through Jesus Christ, the Savior of the world. God's people are sent to be witnesses to and heralds of this wonderful news. In fact, it might be said that one reason God "comes" to us for our own salvation is to "send" us on a mission to be instruments of divine grace in the lives of others.

Moses heard this clearly when God came to him and spoke from the burning bush saying, "I have observed the misery of my people who are in Egypt; I have heard their cry. . . . So come, I will send you to Pharaoh to bring my people, the Israelites, out of Egypt" (Exod. 3:7, 10). Isaiah heard the call that day in the temple when the voice said, "Whom shall I send, and who will go for us?" and he responded, "Here am I; send me!" (Isa. 6:8). And part of Isaiah's message is to remind God's people they are all to be bearers of the light and the gospel. "I am the LORD, I have called you in righteousness, I have taken you by the hand and kept you; I have given you as a covenant to the people, a light to the nations" (Isa. 42:6). Likewise the words of Jesus clearly remind us that we are sent as he was sent (John 20:21) and we are his witnesses to all (Matt. 5:13-16; Acts 1:8).

Although it is difficult not to see this emphasis in the Scripture, it appears quite easy for individuals and congregations to ignore or abdicate this responsibility and assign it by default, if not overtly, to someone else. In most churches, the person seen as responsible for the witness and evangelism work of the church is the pastor. One reason for this is the interesting way the word for "evangelize" gets translated in many English versions of the New Testament.

The Problem of Translation

For example, Philip (selected in Acts 6:5 by the early church to care for the needs of neglected widows) is later called "the evangelist" (Acts 21:8). The only activities of Philip we are able to read about related to his evangelism are described in Acts 8 where all *but* the apostles are scattered from Jerusalem because of persecution (8:1). Philip, and the other "regular" Christians, led of the Holy Spirit, simply went about "evangelizing" (Acts 8:4, 12, 35). Read these passages in almost every English translation and discover that to "evangelize" is constantly translated "to preach" or "to proclaim" the gospel. Even when Philip climbs up into the chariot of the Ethiopian official to have a marvelous one-on-one conversation with him about Jesus, he "preaches" or "proclaims" it according to most of our translations.

When the average Christian or church member today hears the words "preach the gospel" (the usual English translation of the Greek word for "evangelize"), he or she hears only "preach" and says "OK, it must be your job preacher!" Even if smaller churches refer to their clergy as "pastor" or "minister" instead of "preacher" nothing is gained. The problem is that evangelism, often along with much other "ministry," seems to have been clearly labeled by the Holy Bible itself as something accomplished by a single means called "preaching," and a special person ("parson") called the "preacher." Thus, those not called to be preachers, believe they have every good reason to be "off the hook" on evangelism. Such thinking may be largely subconscious, but may be at least one of the reasons why it is often difficult to get persons to sign up for training in evangelism. The image communicated is to "preach" at persons, and most of us intuitively know the best place for this to happen is in church and from the pulpit.[2]

The Problem of Transmission

One of the tragedies in many churches today is that no one is very involved in evangelism. Although almost all congregations have a preacher, most of the preachers see themselves as shepherds of the flock, or chaplains and program managers—not evangelists. In many cases these pastors have received little seminary training or encouragement to be involved in evangelism. Whatever preaching or teaching they engage in is designed much more to instruct and challenge the faithful than to engage and invite a turnaround for "the perishing," "the dying," "the erring," "the fallen," and "tell them of Jesus, the mighty to save."

One painful image of what could happen in some churches, even the "successful" ones, might be found in this Associated Press newspaper article, which appeared several years ago.

NEW ORLEANS—Although 100 lifeguards were present, a fully clothed man drowned at a party to celebrate the first summer in memory without a drowning at a New Orleans city pool.

Jerome Moody, 31, was found on the bottom at the deep end of a

85

New Orleans Recreation Department pool at the end of the party on
Tuesday, recreation department director Madlyn Richard said.

Moody was not a lifeguard and was a guest at the party. Ms.
Richards said he had not been swimming and was fully dressed.

Four lifeguards were on duty at the party and more than half the
200 people there were certified lifeguards, she said.

It was not known when Moody got in the water or how he
drowned.

They pulled him out and tried to revive him until emergency
medical attendants arrived. An autopsy confirmed that he had
drowned.

The goal for churches, as well as other life-protecting-and-saving
institutions, is never merely to have certified personnel on hand, or
to celebrate a glorious history. People in the life-saving business must
always be alert to danger, aware of and sensitive to every person
within their purview, and engaged in their primary work without
distraction. Otherwise, a glorious history can become an ironic
mockery, worn like a millstone around the neck.

Getting Focused for Outreach

In the last chapter we explored the recommendations of turnaround pastors for keeping a congregation on the right path—side-
stepping the obstacles and surviving the dangers and snares. Strange
as it may seem (and it usually does seem strange to smaller churches),
now our objective is to discover how to encourage church members
to risk moving off the path in order that others might find "the Way."
To set the stage, it might be helpful to see what turnaround pastors
answer when asked "What has contributed most to the growth of
this congregation?" Their top twenty answers ranked by frequency
of occurrence are:

Growth Factors in Smaller Churches

1. An atmosphere of love and acceptance
2. Pastoral initiative
3. New programs and outreach ministries
4. Alive, open, inviting worship
5. An attitude of faith and grace

6. A strong Bible focus
7. An emphasis on children and youth
8. Hard work and a desire to grow
9. Inviting friends to church
10. An evangelism emphasis
11. Prayer
12. Emphasis on gifts and discipleship
13. Lay persons involved in visitation
14. Lay persons involved in ministry
15. The blessing of God's Holy Spirit
16. The church location and a growing community
17. Special outreach and evangelistic events
18. Using a strategic planning process
19. Using new people in leadership
20. A pastor willing to stay

It is easy to see by looking at this list that pastors serving smaller churches effective in outreach, evangelism, and growth have a very balanced view of ministry. These pastors are not "narrowly" focused on evangelism. The primary credit for growth is not assigned to a visitation program, even though when asked what they would change if they could in the church's outreach efforts, these pastors indicate "more lay visitation" as their second most often expressed wish. But notice that growth-producing outreach and evangelism in small churches is primarily related to inviting persons to attend warm and exciting experiences of worship (items 1, 4, 5, and 6).

A second cluster of growth factors emerge around new programs and ministries that have an intentional outreach and evangelistic dimension (items 3, 7, and 10). Perhaps item 17 could be included in this category. But it is clear that evangelism and outreach leading to growth in these churches is not primarily a periodic special event. Evangelism that leads to growth is an ongoing effort to contact and invite persons in the community to join with the pastor and members of the church as together they seek God's blessing, love and accept one another, pay attention to God's Word, and witness to the good news of Christ.

One additional group of factors could be collected around the theme of giving new persons a place in the family. Notice especially items 12, 13, 14, and 19. These factors describe a church where lay

TURNAROUND STRATEGIES FOR THE SMALL CHURCH

persons, including newcomers, are being trained and equipped to discover the joy of reaching out to others and giving leadership to the congregation. Together these growth ingredients contribute to a sense of excitement, momentum, and fulfillment for those who have already been reached and who are now identifying themselves as growing disciples of Jesus Christ. More about this in the next chapter, but it should be noted that growth is dependent not only on evangelism defined as reaching out or converting, but also as discipling and developing.

Growth Stages in Smaller Churches

When asked to identify the steps or stages their congregations went through on their way to new life and growth, turnaround pastors indicate they often had to begin with "healing the past" and then move on to "catching the vision" and "finding successful ways to reach new people." Several pastors included a list of five to ten items representing a clear step-by-step approach to renewal and outreach.

> Our stages were: (1) confusion and bickering, (2) power struggle, (3) frustration, (4) a time of decision to be the church instead of a small group of people playing church, (5) adjustment, (6) growth began with new people coming into the church as well as old members coming back, (7) increased vision and outreach.

Another pastor describes the process as working hard with a spouse to reach out to others until the new people coming helped force the changes.

> We visited. We listened. We acted on people's suggestions. The stages we went through were: (1) My wife started a children's program, which reached 47 as we adopted the lessons learned by listening. We were not pushy, but consistently witnessing and present. (2) The children brought their parents. (3) The parents expressed their need and desires. (4) We realized we needed them as much as they needed us. (5) We started programs to reach out. (6) We received visitors warmly. (7) Once they joined we gave them a job to do. (8) We received them into the "inner sanctum" of the church.

88

For one pastor starting over was exactly that. "We closed down the church for nine months and began a Bible study group with new people."

The key ingredient, either before or after healing the wounds and catching the new vision, is the actual experience of success at reaching new people. New faces and families in church enable members to believe again in a brighter future and invest again in their buildings, their witness, and their efforts to please God. When the seventy returned from the mission Jesus sent them on, they "returned with joy" because they had sensed a new power to be effective in Jesus' name (Luke 10:17). Once the twelve or the seventy in smaller churches today experience a similar "success" in reaching out in Jesus's name, they too find a new joy and momentum for ministry.

Efforts to Contact New People

When turnaround pastors are asked to identify their intentional efforts to contact and reach new people, their top fifteen answers are:

1. Emphasize inviting a friend
2. Utilize the phone, letters, ads, signs
3. Start new programs
4. Welcome visitors
5. Encourage lay visitation
6. Followed up visitors
7. Pastoral visitation
8. Focus on children's ministries
9. Deliver welcome packets and baked goods
10. Offer pastoral care to the community
11. Redirect existing programs outward
12. Clarify the meaning of being "Christian"
13. Pray intentionally for unreached people
14. Provide opportunities for new people to serve
15. Plan for special evangelistic events

In and of itself this is a significant collection of outreach strategies for smaller churches. But when the answers to all three outreach and growth questions (growth factors, growth stages, and intentional efforts) are combined with what is known about the pastors themselves, the results are very clear. Successful results in outreach, evangelism, and church growth in smaller churches depend on: (1) having a pastor who leads in evangelism, (2) training, planning and goal setting for growth, (3) inviting friends and family to church, (4) designing programs to reach new people, (5) visiting all prospects, (6) enhancing the church's image through promotion and advertising, (7) holding special evangelistic events, (8) clarifying the meaning of being Christian, (9) praying for God to touch people's lives, and (10) using the gifts of all for the work of the kingdom. The rest of this chapter is dedicated to exploring in more detail the first five items mentioned in the above formula, along with a few observations on the other items thrown in for good measure.

Reaching New People

While sitting at my computer and working on this book, my thirteen-year-old son approached me to ask if I would help him with homework. Like his father, he puts off as long as possible the most challenging assignments. So, twice in one week, late at night, he has asked if I would type for him as he composed an "original story." He talked, I typed. During the sometimes slow and labored process, I wasn't sure if either story was ever going to "arrive." Nevertheless, as the creative juices flowed and special twists were added to each, I began to see a gift I had never noticed before. The stories were brilliant—from a proud father's perspective, of course—and I told him so.

How do we get started in anything that may be a challenge, but could also be part of God's provision for a fuller and more fruitful life? Usually we need both a push and a pull. When Jesus sent out the disciples to carry the gospel of the kingdom to others, they were given an assignment. They were pushed as though by a mother bird, who knew the time had come for them to leave the nest. When we read God's design for us to be witnesses, or hear the words of Jesus describing believers as salt and light, don't we feel the push? Isn't the great commission a push, an assignment, a command? Yet both Jesus and Paul describe the work of the Holy Spirit as an inward longing, a pull toward doing the will of the Father, a love that controls us.

1. Push and Pull Pastors

Which of us would get moving without the outward push? Which of us would keep moving without the upward pull? The greatest, most powerful and creative story ever released won't be written in the lives of others who have never heard it, unless we take it and tell it. But frightened fledglings like ourselves will not get on with it unless we "have to" and then discover we "want to." Pastors who understand this dynamic tension and bring to their congregations both the push and the pull of doing God's will and offering Christ to others, succeed in bringing new life not only to their congregations, but also to their communities.

As noted earlier, nearly 90 percent of these turnaround pastors remember a definite conversion experience of their own and are in pastoral ministry in large part because they want others to know God and find eternal life. They are motivated both by the "pull" of God's love and the possibility of changed lives, as well as by the "push" of obedience to Christ's commands.[3]

Whatever the motivation, evangelism with a view toward church growth is central to the work of turnaround pastors. Richard Zamostny, from Maryland, boldly announces, "I feel all pastors are called to evangelism, and secondly to church growth." Bob Coleman writes from Alabama, "Evangelism is to the church what wet is to water. You can't have one without the other. Evangelism is the church. The church is evangelism." Duane Lewellen maintains:

> Evangelism must be understood as a *natural* thing to do, and not something that is a program of the church. Sharing your faith (or lack of it) is what we do every day without realizing it. Evangelism is simply doing it intentionally in an unobtrusive way. Making people aware of what Jesus has done for them, helps them to share that with others.

David Baldridge asserts "A biblical, Christ-centered church should be involved in growth. Evangelism should be incorporated in all aspects of the church life."

Their approaches to evangelism vary considerably, from door-to-door to working with the poor, but most are involved in their own efforts at evangelizing as well as trying to get their congregations

91

involved. John Kuritz, who was thirty-eight before he entered pastoral ministry, says "I've been telling others about my conversion almost daily since 1958." Even though many wished they had more training in personal evangelism, it was frequently suggested that there was no better way to help others come to faith in Christ than face to face. Others describe their approach more in terms of pastoral involvement in the community such as doing weddings and funerals for unchurched couples and families. Still others speak in terms of preaching and teaching with ample opportunity for people to consider Christ's claims and respond to his invitation either in public worship or in opportunities offered for more private conversations.

These pastors have a deep commitment to evangelism; and wherever they serve, they are going to exercise both the push and the pull approaches to bring their congregations along with them as they reach out to others needing to hear about Christ and belong to his faith community. Their sense of urgency and their personal efforts are contagious. They use whatever seems most appropriate and keep at it until it works. Eric Bell, serving in Alabama, describes the attitude and investment:

> Too many congregations and pastors get the idea that because a community is not growing rapidly, they cannot grow. They give up on their lost neighbors. Last year, a sixty-year-old man was saved, baptized, and united with the church. He had lived in this community most of his life and was not considered "reachable." We can never give up praying, witnessing, and sharing God's love through every means available to win all we can to Jesus Christ. Our church at Trinity has not forgotten that.

2. Training, Planning, and Goal Setting

Pastors committed to fruitful turnaround provide for some kind of training, planning, and goal setting for church growth. Some organize an evangelism or an outreach and mission committee. This team of four to six committed persons meets to discuss their concerns, their dreams, their ideas, and their frustrations. Sometimes they go together to training events held elsewhere, and return home and thoroughly discuss what they heard to determine what seems most appropriate for their circumstances. On occasion they have an outside speaker or a consultant from the denomina-

92

tion or other resource center come meet with them to get them started and encourage their progress. Frequently the pastors themselves have access to materials and a storehouse of ideas, and lead their teams through quite a variety of training experiences. These range from witnessing and preparation for visiting, to full-blown long-range planning and goal setting that is infused with a yearning to reach lost persons.

Robert Vickery, Jr., describes their efforts to reach out saying, "We have classes on witnessing, teaching and receiving." He is training people to talk about their faith, lead classes and Bible studies, and know how to make visitors and newcomers feel warmly welcomed. He continues, "Our people go to seminars elsewhere for training and inspiration. I am training the people to function without a pastor, if necessary. If they are going to survive as a church, they must do the work of the church and not leave it to the pastor."

Sometimes even the most elaborate training efforts seem to be misdirected and/or ineffective. But as some have noted before, shepherds lead their sheep, they don't drive them. One pastor confessed: "All *my* efforts to organize evangelism teams seemed to fizzle, but *they* were already doing the sorts of things needful for effective evangelism. On their own they were inviting and visiting, and they were excited about the church." Training and organization need to be correlated to what the congregation recognizes as an opportunity or a need, and what it accepts as its own way of doing things. Otherwise, the attitude is "If it ain't broke, don't fix it."

What is least complicated and most natural to the understanding of the members will probably garner the most energy and produce the most results. Long-range planning and goal setting have not always fit this description in smaller churches. But several pastors reported significant success with such efforts. Linda Peabody, who pastors in Vernon, Connecticut, held an evangelism workshop with her team of six people using a denominational planning handbook for evangelism ministries. She reports:

Before we began we discussed what we wanted to see happen with this workshop. First, we wanted to feel comfortable evangelizing. Second, more than just going through the exercises of the handbook, we committed ourselves to doing something about it when we were finished. In light of the church's problem of not growing, and in light

93

of our mission to share and spread the Good News with our community and world, we feel that it is extremely important for us, *all of us,* to act upon what we have learned.

They examined their strengths, sought out community needs, and recommended to the congregation five specific steps to be taken to better "share God's Good News through Christ." Once people were clear about what needed to be done, they were ready to give it their very best.

Sometimes the planning begins with analysis. Sometimes it begins with dreaming. Sometimes it is stimulated by setting goals. The most common goal-setting approach is to target a specific percentage of increase in worship attendance and/or membership. Among those who report such percentage goals, the most common is 10 percent growth over the next year. This is an interesting figure since the data on the churches indicate an average membership increase of 56 percent over a five-year period and a 79 percent increase over the same period in worship attendance. Thus, a 10 percent growth goal might be well within reach of most churches.

It appears that setting such goals, planning to reach them, organizing human energy, and training persons in various skills related to evangelism and outreach are important ingredients in effectively reaching out to others and helping smaller churches grow. But the most important single ingredient in a small church's plan for evangelistic effectiveness, according to the pastors surveyed, still centers around what people do most naturally when they are excited about what God is doing in their lives, and that is invite people to church.

3. Inviting Friends and Family

Using natural social networks to reach new people has long been recognized as the most productive method of church growth. Writers in the field have indicated from previous research that larger churches and churches in urban areas grow most readily through using the friendship network. Churches in smaller towns and rural settings, and smaller churches in general have grown more through drawing on family contacts. By a greater than two to one ratio persons answer "Why did you first attend church here?" with "I was invited by a family member." The second most frequent response was "I was invited by a friend or acquaintance." In third place was "looking for a new church," and the fourth most common answer was "a program that met my needs."

Growing smaller churches primarily use an attraction approach to evangelism. When they get together they sense that this is exactly what other people need too, and they become intentional about inviting family members and friends to come to church with them. The best invitations are extended in person—thus the meaning of using the network of "family and friends." But a second way these churches extend the invitation includes contact through advertising and various other methods of community-wide promotion. Posters, brochures, direct mailings, newspapers, newsletters, signs, and even telemarketing have been used by some. Perhaps surprising to some, targeted advertising ranks second only to the emphasis on inviting friends and family.[4]

Samples of brochures and newsletters from turnaround churches include such helpful items of information as: an introduction (name of the church, address, pastor, phone numbers, a motto or brief mission statement, and so on); worship and Sunday school hours; and a list of programs including Sunday school classes, youth and children's activities, Bible studies, communion, men's breakfast, women's fellowships, gospel sings, and a list of any groups regularly using the church buildings for meetings. And always there is an invitation to come join us. Growing smaller churches are doing everything they can to say to the community, "We're here, we're listening, we care, and we want you."

Probably the most productive invitational approach involves designating special Sundays as "Invitation Sundays" or "Friendship Sundays." Some designate one or two Sundays a year, others one Sunday a month as the best day to invite visitors. In either case, this allows for special preparations that could not be made every Sunday including: greeters, a fellowship time with coffee and baked goods, name tags, an easy-to-follow bulletin and order of worship, special music, a straightforward yet sensitive message about the gospel, lay persons prepared to assist in the service, a children's time, no requests for operating funds, a brief testimony or mission moment, cards for visitors to fill out, a visiting team ready to make follow-up calls, a quality special program scheduled that night or the next week to which guests could be invited back, and so on.

One of the most exciting stories of growth among Disciples of Christ in the state of Kentucky is First Christian Church, Albany, which is copastored by Charles and Linda Yarborough who are in their sixties and in their first pastorate. The average attendance at this church during the year before they arrived was twenty-one. On their first Sunday only eighteen were in attendance, and the three youngest were a nine-year-old girl, a four-week-old baby, and her fifty-year-old mother. After two months of getting their bearings, Charles purchased a Friend Day packet and began to prepare the congregation for inviting friends to church. Eight weeks before the Friend Day Sunday he announced the program and told people to begin making plans. Next he formed a committee of a dozen key members. As pastor he wrote to four community leaders and invited them to be his special guests on Friend Day. He informed them that they would be recognized as friends of the community whether they came or not, and that their letters of response would be read to the congregation. Three weeks before the Friend Day their letters of acceptance were read and Charles announced he already had ten or more attending as his guests. All letters of acceptance were posted on a large bulletin board in the narthex.

The next Sunday with two weeks to go the committee was introduced and presented with Friend Day pins. The acceptance letters from their invited guests were read. All members were encouraged by the building momentum and were challenged to "join with us and get involved. All guests are acceptable. Get your friend to sign that he or she will be coming and next week post their notes with ours on the Friend Day board. It's going to be a great day of worship!" It was, and 151 people crowded into the old sanctuary of First Christian Church. It was the first time many could remember that the old faithful members had to select other seats. Thirty-five new prospects were identified and followed up. By repeating the same program twice a year for three years (with a wonderful Harvest Banquet offered in the fall), First Christian Church of Albany, Kentucky, has received fifty new members, thirty-four by baptism, including six teenage boys who joined together on the same Sunday. This church is newly alive and making plans to reach out to even more friends of their community in Christian love.

Variations on this theme are mentioned as the number one method small churches have used to reach out and make new contacts. When these prospects are loved, encouraged, invited back, and offered clear opportunities to make life-changing decisions for Christ, their lives are transformed and so are the churches that invite them.

4. Designing Programs for New People

Developing a sense of mission and a concern for the community often begins when the small church discovers that its buildings can be used for more than Sunday and Wednesday church programs. Occasionally this new "opening" of the church is not much more than providing a place for some community organizations to meet. Duane Waters writes from Florida, "Things started to change when we opened the doors to outside organizations such as Boy Scouts, Girl Scouts, AA meetings, a polling place, etc. We became visible." Other churches reported offering space to such groups as the NAACP, the school board, senior citizens groups, ecumenical programs, parenting groups, and occasionally serving as a crisis center in times of community need.

But opening the church facility to the outside is not the end of the story. Although some churches may settle for being low rent landlords or even a space available charity, growing churches take this "service" at least one step further. They get members involved in working with these groups and identifying with the constituents they serve. The Reverend Waters goes on to say: "One thing that is so very obvious is the amount of time each member is willing to give to volunteer service. My wife now checks blood pressure for anyone who wants it checked the second Sunday of every month, and the third Sunday of the month we open the church and have a covered dish dinner."

The programs used by small turnaround churches to reach out to their communities are myriad. Some are programs common to many churches in lots of communities such as: food pantries, crop walks, tutoring, English as a Second Language classes, sports programs, day care, mothers day out, Twelve Step groups, sewing classes, community Bible studies, vacation Bible school, community choirs, and so forth. But many of the churches developed very special programs to address particular needs and use their gifts in response to God's calling. When these programs were also used as contact points to talk

97

about personal faith and invite people to church, they became important points of entry for new people looking for a place in God's family.

Twenty years ago the Reverend Eduardo Roque arrived to serve the Monte Olivar United Methodist Church in Utuado, Puerto Rico. At that time there were three families and $1.45 in the treasury. Eduardo Roque was a social worker who felt called by God to serve Christ's church. Today the church has over three hundred members in full communion and nearly four hundred in average attendance at the morning worship service. They are no longer small, but in the last few years three new daughter churches have been planted in other suburbs.

The pastor says God has blessed primarily through three "ministries" focused toward the community. First, the church reached out to senior citizens through two women who "offered ambulatory service to five marginated elders of our community." Now twenty-eight volunteers serve over 132 poor senior citizens in the area. They visit them weekly, coordinate their visits to doctors and public agencies, and they celebrate holidays and birthdays together. The second ministry is aimed at children. Twenty-one Extension Bible Schools have been started in various locations with more than 250 children involved. These children not only study the Bible, but also receive counsel and support to become better persons and give themselves in service to others. Third is a program called "The Ministry of Sick Patients." Volunteers give two mornings a week to visit in the hospitals. They feed and bathe the patients as well as offer them and their families emotional and spiritual support. Eduardo Roque reports that the deep concern the congregation now has for evangelism, church growth, stewardship, and theological education began as they reached out to love and serve people all around them.

In 1983 Gil Livingston came to pastor the First Church of God in York, Pennsylvania. Entering ministry late in life he came to this old, downtown church in a changing community with nothing but a strong will, a creative mind, a deep faith, a supportive spouse and twenty faithful worshipers. Along with lots of pastoral visitation in the community and exciting new worship services, programs became very important in reaching new people. The most unusual and original is the "Five F's" program, "Friends For Freedom From

Fear," developed by the Reverend Livingston from the Alcoholics Victorious model, which emerges out of AA.

In the twelve-page brochure printed for the program, the purpose statement includes:

> The Five F's is a group formed to help people with any problem whatsoever, whether caused by such things as chemicals, alcohol, just plain selfishness, or what have you. . . . We come together at our meetings to offer support to each other in our fight against our problems, and to accept that support as a part of the healing process, Galatians 6:2 ("Bear one another's burdens, and in this way you will fulfill the law of Christ"). We firmly believe that supporting each other with God supporting the whole, we will remain free. Any person who has a problem, or is related to one who has a problem, is welcome to join us. The only condition for entering the group is that the person is sincere in wanting help.

In addition to the Five F's program, First Church has designed a Wednesday JOY Bible Club for children and several other programs for men and women. The twenty in worship has now risen to over 120 in two morning worship services. These new persons were primarily reached through quality programs addressing special needs in people's lives.

Although several kinds of programmatic outreach become important to smaller turnaround churches, the most frequently mentioned involve children and youth. Again and again pastors write: "We started classes for children and youth and targeted young families. There were only 13 children in the church six years ago, and now we average over 60 in Sunday school every week."

To reach the youth and children the churches use existing programs such as Sunday school and VBS, as well as starting new programs such as Scouts, day care, youth fellowships, and special music and drama groups. In our study the average percentage increase in children involved in programs of the church and especially in Sunday school was 121 percent in five years. The average number of children for all churches surveyed was thirty-five. The average increase in youth involvement was 133 percent with an average of fourteen youth involved.

Many leaders at small churches have confused themselves by

99

thinking that they are too small, that they do not have enough people, to run a program. They may be unable to offer a full-service approach, but tremendous personal and social problems still keep many people from even hearing of the freedom Christ offers because they don't yet believe that the church really cares or that it has any balm to offer. Unchurched Americans often believe the church's only product is judgmental morality or perhaps insurance for the life to come. How will people near our churches discover the salvation Christ provides for this life as well as the life to come unless we find ways to reach into their worlds instead of waiting for them to come to ours? Small turnaround churches using programs to reach out are discovering what Jesus meant when he said "As the Father has sent me, so I send you" (John 20:21), "Go therefore and make disciples" (Matt. 28:19), and "Let the little children come to me; do not stop them; for it is to such as these that the kingdom of God belongs" (Mark 10:14).

5. Visiting All the Prospects

In the introduction to *Growing Plans*, Lyle Schaller wrote: "Despite this plethora of creative ideas and programs, the best single approach still is the old-fashioned system of personal visitation."[5] After describing further his rationale for this strong affirmation, Schaller acknowledges that nevertheless many churches find this approach difficult or inappropriate.

Sometimes the pastors themselves are not particularly comfortable with the idea. But more often members who have lived in the community for many years frequently resist risking their relationships with neighbors and acquaintances through what they perceive to be an unnatural "intrusion" approach to witnessing. On the other hand, many pastors and congregations have had exciting results and affirming responses from almost all persons contacted. Perhaps much of the difference is in attitude and people skills as well as how the effort is modeled and communicated.

One way not to promote a visitation program appeared in the bulletin of a Rochester, Pennsylvania church. "The outreach committee has enlisted 25 visitors to make calls on people who are not afflicted with any church." If the typist was subconsciously or otherwise expressing his or her real convictions, the visitation team was in for a rough time of it. Even if people came, why would they want to stay?

Generally, pastors serving turnaround congregations indicate lay visitation and pastoral visitation are very important methods for contacting new people. For some, especially many of the pastors themselves and sometimes their spouses, this means calling on those identified as inactive or unchurched, as well as visiting in hospitals, nursing homes, and even door to door in some communities, just to get acquainted and extend an invitation to church. Much more common, however, the visitation programs are described as "people who take cookies (pies, loaves of bread, cakes) to the visitors," and "a follow-up phone call by one of our members before Thursday." Some feel they already have a minimal level program in place, but indicate "We need to expand our present program and include same day follow-up visits with a plant, a brochure, and a 'thank you for coming.'" Or, as another pastor said, "We need more people to: (1) do follow-up visits to visitors, (2) visit the sick and shut-ins, (3) visit members on key days (death in family, birthday, anniversary), and (4) visit new families in area."

One very encouraging story was shared about Steven's Hill Community Church of the Brethren in rural Pennsylvania.

The Steven's Hill Church had struggled for years. I wasn't around in those days, but they say that the constant bickering between two families had prevented the church from growing. Two and a half years ago the decision was made to close the doors.

A man named Bill Longenecker felt called of the Lord to reopen the church. Bill is a 61-year-old sheep farmer who has served as an evangelist and an interim pastor in several churches over the years. With the blessings of the district, Bill began visiting in the community and started a Bible study with some of the remnant of the congregation and several new people. Bill recruited another well-grounded couple to assist him in his visitation and by October the Bible study group had grown to more than twenty.

As the story continues several began to talk about reopening the church. They worked to make improvements on the old building and decided to use an aerial map and visit every home within two miles of the church. The estimate was about two hundred homes. In reality there were more than seven hundred. As of the writing of the letter,

101

they had visited more than four hundred homes. Tim and Beth Shenk, active members, describe the results.

A year and a half later our attendance has grown to over seventy on a Sunday morning, 80 percent of whom were not active in a church a year ago. Many of the people in our church are baby boomers who grew up in the church, but stopped attending for various reasons. We have contacted homes as many as ten times before families have come to church the first time. We always fear that we will turn people off with our repeated visits and calls, but that does not seem to be the case. We've found that it's often helpful to have different people visit the same household. That way, before they come to church, they already know several people.

To sum up, we attribute the success of the Steven's Hill church to the guidance of the Holy Spirit, persistent visitation, a good Sunday school and nursery, a friendly atmosphere, and sound biblical preaching.

Sometimes success in visitation is related to the community, but many of the pastors themselves admit they are still adjusting and learning how to make the best evangelistic visits. Some, like Bill Longenecker, have experience in serving as evangelists, or have been trained in programs such as Evangelism Explosion, or have benefited from working with various evangelistic organizations. But many feel inadequately prepared themselves to know how to lead another person to Christ, and thus have little inclination to train lay persons to become more effective visitors and witnesses.

One of the most encouraging stories was shared by Val Hastings, Jr. who is a United Methodist pastor in Pennsylvania. After finishing his M.Div. degree and pastoring for five years he says,

I was scared to death that someone might ask me, "How do I become a Christian?" or "What are the basic Christian beliefs?" I was convinced that I could answer most of their questions using theological language from seminary, but I didn't know if I could translate into the language of the average person. I talked with my District Superintendent who suggested I go to Ft. Lauderdale and attend an Evangelism Explosion seminar for pastors and use whatever I could. I was actually shocked when for the first time in my life a person said "Yes, I'd like to make this decision."

Following this training, the Reverend Hastings offered a two-hour seminar to some of his members and claims it was a milestone. After moving to another parish he trained first one and then another to work with him and follow up Sunday visitors every Sunday evening. Soon four people were involved, two visiting with the pastor, and two staying behind at the church to pray. He reports it became a wonderful experience for those on both sides of the task. Now there are eight involved. A very important aspect of their training is the emphasis on learning to tell the gospel using everyday words and not a lot of "church language." They have also been learning how to use various questions to get deeply into spiritual matters. These include: "On a scale of one to ten, how would you rate your life?" and "If you were to meet Jesus today walking down the street, and he said why should I accept you, what would you say?"

Perhaps the best summary of the impact of this program on the church is caught in an article appearing in the Conference newsletter.

On April 28, 1991, Emmanuel UMC of Brownstown went over the 200 mark for the first time in 20 years. Over the last two years this "small" church has received over 50 new members. "We're not only excited about our increase in membership," says the pastor, "but also in our weekly attendance at worship, which has doubled in two years."

When asked how this all happened, Don Eckert (PPR chairperson) says, "Much of our success is because of our visitation program. Two years ago we began plans to start Evangelism Explosion. Visitors at worship, new residents and new children in Sunday School are all visited by Evangelism Teams. Over half of the people we visit come back to our church and eventually join our church family."[6] The Reverend Hastings reports that few make decisions the first time they are visited or hear the gospel explained in very personal terms that invite a response. But as the months pass and people have additional opportunities to hear this challenge, be loved by the congregation, and feel the tug of the Holy Spirit on their souls, they joyfully respond and become committed members of the church.

Here is an exciting, growing, revitalized, evangelistic congregation whose members are learning the importance of visiting and actually talking to others about Jesus Christ and the difference he can make in human lives. Although visitation ministries take many different forms in these churches, there is no question about the benefit of face-to-face contact, conversation, and prayer with people who are seeking to find their way to God and invest their lives in kingdom work.

Offer Them Christ

Effective Christian witness involves many forms of mission and ministry, but the core of our witness is still that message of salvation and hope, which no other organization can offer. The heartbeat of every Christian congregation must be reflected in the words "offer them Christ" if it can call itself alive and well. Much more could be reported about particular programs and approaches used by small churches to reach out to their communities, but we have seen the results of pastors and churches who have caught the vision and invested their energies in faithfully reaching out to turn things around in the lives of those who are faltering.

It may be time in your church for a little prayerful soul searching as congregations ask themselves "What are we trying to do for heaven's sake?"

VI

TURNAROUND LEADERS DEVELOP DISCIPLES

They devoted themselves to the apostles' teaching and fellowship, to the breaking of bread and the prayers.
Acts 2:42

Even a once-over-lightly reading of the New Testament reveals that the gospel of the kingdom of God is about something more than mere rescue. The goal is nothing short of complete restoration, a new creation, which begins with rescue. Jesus himself summarizes it in words often causing problems for theologians and debaters: "Be perfect, therefore, as your heavenly Father is perfect" (Matt. 5:48). The task of the church, regardless of its size, is to be faithful to the work of Christ in the life of every believer, to the end that, "rooted and grounded in love," we might live lives worthy of being called children of God.

The natural inquiry to follow the emphasis on outreach and evangelism addressed in the last chapter is: "How do the pastors of turnaround churches enable their members to mature in the faith, exercise their gifts for ministry, and become true disciples of Jesus Christ?" Although the question can be worded several ways, it would be a mistake to think the answer is only a matter of changing individuals. The goal is also to shape congregations into mature manifestations of Christ's body.

The purpose of this chapter is to: (1) examine the role of pastoral leadership in the process of maturation, (2) identify the stages involved as a congregation moves from dream to mission, and (3) explore some ideas for producing a congregation of maturing disciples involved in ministry.

Pastoral Leadership for Change

Three leadership priorities can be identified as foundational for pastors of smaller churches who lead their congregations through the transitions into new life as effective centers of Christian ministry. The first is the almost unconscious value they place on momentum. Like coaches of athletic teams, they realize that everything cannot be changed all at once, but that without a sense of momentum there will be little chance of defeating the demon of discouragement. Their second priority is flexibility, or what has sometimes been called situational leadership. They readily shift from one style or function of leadership to another as required by the situation at hand and/or how far along the congregation is in its transition to a fully functioning center of ministry. Third, their leadership is shaped by the belief that the ultimate goal is full transformation of persons and the congregation itself into manifestations of God's grace and glory.

1. Leadership as Momentum

Two former students, both entering the ministry in midlife, returned from "working the fields" as pastors of smaller churches and came by for a chat. One was packing up his family and leaving a church after his first year. He was discouraged and felt he needed training in "spiritual warfare." He had become snarled in a family feud and felt forced to decide what the church's stand was going to be on a very controversial subject. He bit the bullet, took his stand, served as the prophetic voice of truth, denounced the sin, and was asked to leave. Perhaps the Spirit will use his sacrificial boldness and the church will benefit from this challenge, but there is no way to know.

The other pastor was finishing his third year at his church and glowed as he told of loving and being loved, of reaching people for Christ, and of watching new leadership emerge in a church full of octogenarian gatekeepers. He too was leaving to take a new church, but full of excitement that God was doing a new thing and that real change had taken place. Both pastors loved their people, both loved Christ, both wanted to make a difference, both did. But the differences they made are themselves quite different.

When it comes to pastoral leadership that makes the difference called "turnaround," is it primarily a matter of "the luck of the draw" or "providence"? Not usually, although some churches need much more healing than others. Do successful pastors get good churches to start with? No, rather they learn to or intuitively know how to walk through minefields and come out on the other side. They choose their battles carefully and don't let others force them into corners. They realize that change comes slowly as Christ, not the pastor, becomes recognized as the head of the body, and as love matures and makes fertile the soil of growth.

Was one of the pastors described above wrong and the other right? No. Did one have it easy and the other have it hard? No. But one may have worked more wisely and made choices with an eye toward the big picture and the long haul. The other chose to resolve a single issue; and although he boldly spoke the truth and drew a line in the sand, he lost the right to continue speaking. He had become the judge, so he was no longer able to pastor. He came to believe that "combat" is the proper description of ministry. The other described it as "embracing change with love." One focused on the fight, the other on the future.

These differences are not absolute, but even Jesus knew his ministry was larger than simply being the "lamb of God." He had a mission to accomplish with the twelve and with his other disciples. He spoke boldly, but he also cautioned against judging. He knew when to withdraw as well as when to enter the Temple and combat the money changers. Conflict will come; but pastors who create new futures for their congregations seem to understand and practice "timing." They function more from a mindset committed to completing the vision than to announcing truth and settling disputes. They realize momentum is easily sidetracked. Therefore, whenever pos-

107

sible, they stick with their plan and their calling, and avoid pitfalls that lead to divided loyalties and win/lose contests of authority.

2. Leadership as Flexibility

Turnaround pastors describe their top six leadership functions as (1) visionary, (2) enabler/encourager, (3) partner/friend, (4) facilitator, (5) cheerleader, and (6) transformational leader. Although the question did not ask for multiple answers, many seemed to understand that being successful as a visionary—enabling the vision to become a reality—requires multiple leadership functions. Some approaches are more helpful in the early days of change, others are more appropriate in the stages that follow. Effective leadership committed to momentum adjusts as the conditions dictate.

Several indicated they initially functioned more as visionaries, initiators, and cheerleaders, but later shifted to become teachers, administrators, and equippers. One pastor confesses "I'm mostly a democratic leader, but sometimes I have leaned toward 'benevolent dictator' to initiate change." Another writes: "My roles have changed from being an initiator and solo staff person to becoming an equipper and leader of volunteer staff. Once I had to do almost everything, now I am primarily a vision leader and teacher." These pastors seem to understand that appropriate leadership is what is needed at the moment for the sake of momentum. Their leadership is flexible, not a single style or predefined role or function that will remain the same while everything else around it changes.

Flexibility in style of leadership has been studied by a number of researchers in the management and human development field. Paul Hersey and Kenneth Blanchard developed a model in 1976 they called "Situational Leadership," which calls for various blends of relational support and task instruction based on the ability and willingness of the workers. Our use of the word *flexibility* is not identical to the concept of situational leadership as described by Hersey and Blanchard, but it is similar.

Perhaps Jesus exercised a form of situational leadership with his disciples. He began his ministry with the twelve disciples by teaching them and showing them what was required in kingdom ministry (Luke 5–8). As their understanding of the task and their intimate relationship with Jesus increased, he sent them out on their own to try their wings at kingdom ministry (Luke 9:1-9). They returned to him and discussed and evaluated all they had experienced (Luke 9:10). Later, seventy are reported to be sent on a similar mission and return to reflect with Jesus on the success of the mission and to celebrate the results (Luke 10:1-20). Finally, John reports that Jesus told his disciples it would be better for them if he departed so that the Holy Spirit could come to be their guide and comforter (John 16:7-13). Although his love for them remained constant, the way Jesus led his band of followers was flexible, depending on their needs and their readiness for responsibility.

Successful shepherds of his flock today seem to follow their master's example. They understand the big picture and accept their place in it as a key to change, but they realize that they have different roles to play as momentum is established and the congregation progresses through various stages of revitalization on the way to maturity. "Everyone mature in Christ" can be called a transformational goal, and leaders committed to this goal are transformational leaders.

3. Leadership as Transformation

Many studies have been done on leadership, and nearly 150 definitions of the term have appeared in print. But one of the more helpful recent typologies of leadership is that offered by historian and political scientist, James MacGregor Burns. Burns first described the difference between *transactional* and *transformational* leadership.[1] Transactional leaders want clear lines of authority and power, and function in terms of an exchange, or a transaction. They want their followers satisfied, but mostly in order to fulfill their own personal goals of success. Their approach is "You give me something and I'll give you something." Robert Cueni suggests in his book *The Vital Church Leader* that a pastor functioning as a transactional leader might offer "God's grace in exchange for a healthy contribution, or encourage people to unite with the church as a way to enhance their social standing and to build the pastor's evangelism record."[2] At best, transactional leaders think in terms of fulfilling the contract, being successful, and doing the job for which they were hired. At worst, they focus only on measurable outcomes, they accumulate power, they seek to promote dependency, and they try to reduce the influence of others so they can control every situation. Transactional leaders can become highly manipulative, impersonal, and even exploitative.

Transformational leadership is based on mutual enhancement, not a one-for-one exchange that is developed out of self-interest. The goal of transformational leaders is to inspire followers to a higher level of participation and satisfaction. They serve as moral agents who facilitate change while encouraging and elevating others to greater levels of responsibility. They are often described as movers and shakers, visionaries, intellectual leaders, leaders of reform, innovators, and even heroes.[3]

This is the type of leadership best exercised by turnaround pastors. They are investing in people and in a vision. They adjust to the changing needs of their congregations and their communities. Their pleasure is not in securing a name for themselves, but in seeing others grow and become empowered and excited about serving Christ. They try to adjust their own roles and styles of leadership based on the needs of others. They seek to elevate followers into leaders and enable all to function as true Christian disciples. This is their vision for the churches they serve, and this is what they commit themselves to with all the faith, hope, and love they can offer.

Sharon Patch, pastoring in Florida, entered the ministry in midlife. It is easy to see her transformational vision for ministry when she writes:

> God has given me gifts that can be used effectively in proclaiming the gospel and I desire above all else to help others know God's love and transforming power. I long to see the body of Christ grow and thrive.

O. Phillip May, a second career pastor in Arkansas, reveals a similar commitment to partnership in ministry and being a leader among leaders.

> I defined myself as a leader in worship and a partner in ministry. I wrote, taught, and preached positively without being autocratic or dictatorial. I invited response and expected leadership of the laity.

These pastors, many of whom have sacrificed comfort, professional status, and financial security to follow God's call, are in the ministry not because they see it as a way "up" for themselves, but because they long with all their hearts to see others succeed and be transformed. They are transformational leaders.

4. Put Them All Together

Although we have been describing three priorities in the leadership styles of pastors acknowledged as successful change agents, the priorities are not entirely separate from one another. In reality and in practice, they overlap considerably and interact with one another to produce what might be called simply pastoral leadership for revitalized congregations.

James Kouzes and Barry Posner have collaborated to produce a description of the behaviors and commitments of those they label exemplary leaders.[4] Their list of practices closely resembles the activities and values described by the pastors in our study. According to Kouzes and Posner, exemplary leaders:

1. **Challenge the process**—seek out new opportunities, are pioneers, innovate, experiment, take risks, and view mistakes as learning experiences.
2. **Inspire a shared vision**—look toward but beyond the horizon, are hopeful, positive, expressive, genuine, good communicators, build on mutual interests toward a common purpose, and enlist support from others.
3. **Enable others to act**—nurture relationships based on mutual trust and respect, involve others in planning and decisions, foster collaboration, and work to strengthen others.
4. **Model the way**—are clear about their own values and beliefs, model the behavior they expect from others, plan thoroughly, clarify achievable steps, and create opportunities for small wins and achievable goals.
5. **Encourage the heart**—recognize accomplishments and contributions, express appreciation and pride, celebrate achievements, nurture team spirit, and thus inspire continued efforts to work for the vision.

111

From Vision to Mission

How do these pastors lead their congregations from the earliest steps of affirmation, encouragement, and dreaming, through whatever it takes to become transformed into exciting centers of ministry and mission? Their answers are not all the same, but three key elements keep recurring: (1) they have their own personal vision for the church, (2) they encourage the dreams of others and facilitate a common vision for the church's future, and (3) they develop a purpose-driven church through some form of strategic planning.

1. They Have a Dream

In one of the cartoons by Charles Schultz, Lucy has enticed Charlie Brown into a conversation by reducing her rates for "Psychological Help" from 25 cents to a nickel per hour. Lucy opens the dialogue.

"Charlie Brown, Life is like a cruise ship. On the Cruise Ship of Life there are deck chairs you can move around."

Charlie focuses in as she continues: "Some people take their deck chairs and place them on the front of the ship. They are hopeful. They always want to see where they are going. Others find comfort in the past and they like to place their deck chairs on the stern of the ship."

Then the big question: "Charlie Brown, on the Cruise Ship of Life, where would you put your chair?"

Charlie Brown's face gets that wrinkled look made famous by Charles Schultz, and he replies, "I just can't seem to get my deck chair unfolded."

Pastors leading revitalized smaller churches recognize this scenario. Without exception, they would unfold their chairs up front. As Lucy says, "They are hopeful," and "want to see where they are going." Actually, they also invest a great deal of time and energy helping others get their chairs unfolded, and then call as many as will follow to move with them to the bow of the ship. Occasionally they visit with those who prefer the stern, and they celebrate the memories of times and places left behind; but as captains of the ship they believe the most important view is toward what is coming, not toward what has been.

By no means do all of these pastors start their first conversation with the announcement "Come to the front of the ship!" but some do. In fact, one pastor in Los Angeles, Sylvester Gillespie, wrote a

112

two-page open letter to the officers and members of the church he had been appointed to, informing them of his approach to ministry and his dream for the church even *before* he arrived for his first Sunday. Included in the letter were the following thoughts:

How does Pastor Gillespie view his members? You are not someone to do my thing on, you are my thing. You will never be an interruption of my work, but are the purpose of my work. My mission is clear as outlined by Jesus when he said to Simon Peter, "If you love me, feed my sheep." There is no room in the Church of Jesus Christ for some members to get special treatment over others. Every name on the roll of the church is a very special person whether he/she is a disgruntled member, a member who has left the church, a member with a grammar school education, or a member with a Ph.D.

Therefore:

1. I am not interested in negative news about others.

2. I am not interested in how much experience, prestige or power one has unless these things are tied into and in concert with Jesus Christ governing our decisions.

3. I am not interested in where we are now, or where we were five weeks, five months, or five years ago, but where God can lead us to from here.

It is not enough just to trust God to get things moving. For new things to come to pass we must act on the trust we claim we have. We can soar to new heights by being bold, brazen, and daring in Jesus Christ.

The pastoral letter continued and established the centrality of the Bible, called for a churchwide conference, announced the start of a new second worship service at 8:00 A.M. Sunday mornings, and requested the hanging of a new, colorful, professionally printed banner declaring "Grace United Methodist Church, The Church Where Jesus is the Star, and the Bible has Center Stage." And in closing, Pastor Gillespie instructed the members that he would be calling on all sick and homebound members immediately, and that he wanted to organize the membership of the church into a caring network of "classes."

Although few pastors would use this "jump start" approach to help clarify their own personal vision, almost all describe from the earliest days of their arrival the importance of their own dreams and visions for their churches. Another pastor writes:

113

I walked into that little run-down church where they paid me thirty-five dollars a week and I saw a holy place which God had given me to have a ministry. You have to dream God's dream. See the "beauty" in the "beast" and they will act beautiful. A positive pastor in a negative church can turn it around in three years. A negative pastor in a positive church can destroy it in three months.

I never saw a church empty. I always saw it full.

Pastors who make a difference have a dream and see a vision of the way things can be. They don't deny the way things are, but they exude a confidence about the way things are going to be.

2. They Facilitate a Common Vision

When effective pastors lead from their own visions, they are energized for ministry. But for an entire congregation to be energized for ministry requires the dream and the vision to be caught and shared by all—or at least by a group of key "movers and shakers." So, how do these pastors engender a common vision?

First and foremost they talk about, pray about, and preach about the vision they believe in. They remind people "The best days of the church are always ahead, not behind." And they function from the premise that the only worthy dream or vision for a church needs to be based "on God's ability, not human ability." Billy Strayhorn, a United Methodist pastor in Texas seems to use this approach. He writes:

> The former pastor left in an angry tirade. I came with humor and joy, talking about dreams and vision. At first there was disbelief. But the people caught the vision and started inviting friends and acquaintances, and we budgeted for growth. We started Sunday school classes without any students so that when they showed up, they would have a class.

Perhaps this is what the writer of Hebrews had in mind when writing: "Now faith is the assurance of things hoped for, the conviction of things not seen" (11:1).

Some of the dreaming and visioning in these churches is mostly a matter of regaining a sense of hope and power, more a matter of a new "image" than a written statement. But many of the pastors

114

actually help their people create a statement. Dennis Hamshire helped the Green Street Church of God in Harrisburg, Pennsylvania, create a "Dream Statement," which envisions their church "being the focal point of our community in terms of meeting needs; filled with people; helping young people carry forth the faith; keeping our facility attractive, used to its maximum potential, and expanded as necessary to respond to growth and to meet needs."

Sometimes the vision is recorded more like a motto for the quality of ministry or the type of church the congregation wants to be known for than as a formal statement. Two examples are: "Making room for our neighbors in the fellowship of faith" and "A warm church that shows the love of God and ministers to all people in a fresh New Testament atmosphere."

Such expressions of a congregation's dream or vision are not purpose statements or mission statements, but they are related. First a congregation begins to see itself and its future through the eyes of faith and hope, then it can engage in more specific planning and goal setting. The initial congregational vision for a small church in the midst of revitalization is not necessarily the end product of strategic planning. More likely it is only the firstfruits. But as some of the sweetness of new life is savored, the congregation is often ready for the additional planning needed for an even greater harvest.

3. They Develop a Purpose-Driven Church

The most important step in the success of this process is clarifying the congregational purpose. This is carried over from the dreaming and visioning efforts already mentioned, and is where both the Bible and the prayerful discussions of the members meet. The primary goal is to find answers to questions like the following: "Who are we?" "Why are we here?" "Whose church is this anyway?" "What does God expect of us?" "What is our special identity and contribution to this community?" "Where is our future?" "How can we be faithful to our heritage in a new day?" "Who are the people God desires us to be responsible for?" "How will we witness for Christ?" "What are we expecting God to do among us in the days ahead?"

Some pastors begin by asking such questions informally to key people in their congregations, just to get the ball rolling. Some establish a special committee to work on this task after gathering congregational input and census data or other community information. But almost all believe that finding their identity and God's purpose for them in the Bible is most important. Many denominational planning resources as well as books on church leadership offer models for arriving at and writing a purpose statement. Some of these statements are quite elaborate, but most are a few carefully chosen phrases or sentences addressing such areas as: worship, witness, outreach, nurture, discipleship, stewardship, and caring for the needs of others. These sometimes are identical to what a congregation calls its "Mission Statement" although a mission statement may be more specific and adjusted from year to year as opportunities and conditions change.

A purpose-driven church: (1) builds morale by reducing the tension of competing claims; (2) reduces frustration because it helps prioritize and clarify what needs to be done; (3) builds cooperation among those inside the church and attracts the interest and cooperation of persons and groups outside the church; and (4) assists in regular evaluation of congregational faithfulness and effectiveness.[5]

After helping the congregation to clarify its purpose, turnaround pastors employ various methods of setting goals, solving problems, and planning for change. Planning, at least extensive planning, is not one of the natural things that a small congregation does. Small churches are like families, and families normally live from day to day unless a problem comes up. There may be a savings account for the "rainy day," but seldom do families sit down together and write out their dreams, their specific and attainable goals, and their annual and five-year plans. Most small churches prefer to take things as they come. It is not at all unusual around smaller churches to hear the following sympathies expressed: "Planning is for those larger corporations and businesses, not for families; and here at Love Your Neighbor Church, we really are like a family."

Although such thinking may be natural and rooted in a long history, turnaround churches and their pastors are involved in change; change not merely as something happening to them, but change they intend by God's grace to bring about. "Strategic Planning" sounds much more grandiose than some of the actual efforts may warrant, but even the smallest and most informal churches seem to be thinking intentionally about the future and putting flesh on the bones of their dreams. They are setting goals and making plans for changes to their facilities and for new programs and evangelistic efforts.

Some pastors, like Ruth Simmons of Parkersburg, West Virginia, use a fairly simple problem-solving approach. She writes:

> My leadership style at first was to present a problem and allow the people to develop a strategy to deal with it. At first they would have no idea where to begin, so I would quickly lay out three or four alternatives. They would discuss them and come up with one. Now, *they* present different ways to solve the problems.

Others have gone through more formal strategic planning processes involving annual planning retreats, printed reports, and even outside consultants. One church, Otterbein United Methodist Church in Warren, Ohio, even creates an annual "Manual for Ministry." The first page of one of their recent manuals includes the following gems:

MINISTRY THEME: "Heart and Hands for Christ"

INTRODUCTION: "Goals are dreams which have gotten dressed in workclothes." This *Manual For Ministry* represents the dreams, ideas, concerns, and needs that God is bringing before us through each other. "Dreams" are God's gifts offering us His invitation to share God's continuing creative acts in the lives of people. We celebrate God's dreams through us as God's people. We affirm that: "Failing to plan is planning to fail."

DEFINITIONS: 1. *Mission*—discovery of needs based upon the biblical principles revealed through the ministry of Jesus Christ (5 Areas).

2. *Objective*—a bridge to action, ideas formed into plans that guide "dreams" toward fulfillment in accordance with the biblical principles from God's Word within and through us.

3. *Target*—where the rubber meets the road; God's Word and will fleshed out through assignments and accountabilities of persons, dates, places, and costs/funding sources.

Jim Vander Slik serves a fairly new Christian Reformed congregation in Florida and uses his extensive background in business to lead congregational planning. He says his approach is trying "to present 'fork in the road' choices to people, encouraging them to make the right choice." The Sunday worship program (bulletin) includes a purpose statement labeled "Concept of Ministry." In addition, three congregational "Spiritual Goals" are listed to help both the existing members and new people remember and understand where the church is headed.

These pastors seem to know how and when to shift from the more informal dreaming and visioning so necessary to establish a positive view of the future, to the more formal purpose and mission statements, and finally to specific, measurable, and attainable goals. Not all approach this journey from "vision to mission" in the same manner, but the very fact that they succeed in leading their congregations into new ministry efforts and congregational growth indicates that these pastors are not just visionaries and dreamers. They know how to help people see the implications of their dreams, clarify their God-given purpose, and "put on the workclothes" of goals and planning.

Developing a Congregation of Maturing Disciples

Kouzes and Posner, in listing the five behaviors and commitments of "exemplary leaders," indicate that they enable others to act and model the way. Pastors of turnaround smaller churches have a deep commitment as transformational leaders to developing leadership in others. In addition, they highly value the biblical mandate to "make disciples" and they define success in terms of developing mature disciples as well as reaching out to make new disciples. From the first moment new believers or transferring members are welcomed into the fellowship of these churches, they indicate that they feel at home and yet challenged to give of their best and discover the joy of living life at a new level.

What do the pastors of these churches do to help this happen? First, they know how to create a special atmosphere of warmth and welcome in God's grace. Second, they emphasize Christian discipleship and the process involved in growing up into all we are meant to be as mature Christians. Third, they believe in discovering and employing each person's gifts for ministry. Fourth, they understand the need for creative interaction between larger gatherings of the whole congregation and small groups for nurture and growth.

Finally, they help their members discover how to live and how to serve God in the larger world.

1. Create an Atmosphere of Welcome

Perhaps it is only natural that pastors who see their second and third most important gifts for ministry—after preaching—as "loving people" and having "people skills" should be able to make newcomers and old-timers alike feel wanted and welcomed. But any of us who have been in these situations realize it is not easy. Long-term members sometimes feel they are losing control with the arrival of new people and they do not always communicate a warm welcome. Even persons who sincerely say, "How good it is to have you with us!" sometimes only speak the words and aren't sure what actions are needed to make the sounds become a song. Welcoming new people is not easy, and it uses up psychological energy, even for those who love company.

One reason for the difficulty is that church visitors and new members in small churches are not merely "company" or "guests," as it is sometimes put in megachurches. Rather, they are potential or actual new family members waiting to be adopted.[6] Making company feel welcome is a much different and less threatening task than adopting new family members. New members bring their own set of problems still to be worked out; and most families feel they already have enough of their own.

It might be reassuring to look again at Acts and Paul's letters to notice that all was not smooth and wonderful in the early church. Some particular passages to note are: Acts 5:1-11; 6:1-7; 15 including verses 36-41; Rom. 14:1–15:13; 1 Cor. 1:10-31; chapters 12, 13, and 14; 2 Cor. 5:12–6:1; Eph. 4; Phil. 2. Why did Jesus pray so intently for our unity (John 17:20-24), and why did Paul write so often about love, oneness in the Spirit, and welcoming one another if it was so easy? In fact, when it did happen, it was its own kind of "miracle" and convinced many of the priests (Acts 6:7) to join in this new faith. The same sign of God's power seems to be at work today in churches that have leaders who work hard to help create the welcome that is needed.

From the initial contact with new people multiple efforts are made to help them feel wanted. They find a building that looks clean, cared

119

for, and ready for visitors; sometimes they even find a special "Visitor" parking space right near the door; attractive signs give good and accurate information, and colorful bulletin boards display pictures of "New Members" and achievements to celebrate; people go out of their way to introduce themselves and visitors are introduced to everyone as the worship service begins; during worship they experience a warm, engaging friendship between the pastor and the members, they hear good news from the Bible and sincere prayers for people's needs; they observe that members of the congregation help lead worship as well as occupy the pews; after the service they are invited to other events, classes, choirs, and sometimes even to lunch; in the days following they are visited by lay persons, the pastor, or both; gifts representing "family love" (pies, cookies, fresh bread, flowers) are taken by; perhaps they receive a phone call or cards, notes, letters, special brochures, and newsletters are sent; and they are remembered by name the next time they visit. Not bad for starters.

As new people continue to attend worship and perhaps other church activities, they are visited by the pastor or invited to a new members class to discuss the meaning of being Christian, baptism, and joining the church. Most of the pastors indicate they have from one to three personal conversations with those interested in joining, or from four to six weeks of classes. When new people do decide to profess their faith and join, they already feel accepted and part of the family. On the occasion of their baptism and/or their membership in the church, the event is not merely a formal exercise of two minutes' duration, but a celebration. One church pulls out all the stops and sends formal invitations to a special "white tablecloth and best china" dinner where the new members are warmly "roasted" and presented personalized leather-bound Bibles with their names inscribed in gold leaf.

When we love as God loves, it isn't hard to use our creative imaginations and be a little lavish as we throw a wedding party and celebrate new births, new life, new family members, and the mystery of union in love between Christ and his Bride. Small churches actually have a much easier time with this than large churches. It is one of the truly wonderful things about being just the right size to welcome everyone up close and personal.

2. Emphasize Discipleship

Hazel Porter is a pastor in Jacksonville, Florida, and believes it is always appropriate to remind people of our central purpose as Christ's church. She writes: "It is important to be intentional about one's relationship to Jesus Christ. I always start a meeting with this question: 'How can we serve Christ's call to make disciples?'" Disciples follow Jesus. What do we need in the way of Bible study, devotional disciplines, loving and supportive community, reorientation of our limited worldviews, resources, and training to be able to follow where he is leading today? These are the issues and the language often used in churches where new members are kept alive not simply to serve a status quo institution, but to be part of a movement of the kingdom of God.

Although discipleship is not the only way to describe and emphasize this dynamic understanding of Christian living, it does avoid some passive images regarding church membership. Barbara Florey is a United Methodist pastor in Michigan and says, "This next year I'm going back through my preaching plan and I am going to preach the whole year on discipleship. I want to get over using the word *volunteer* and start using the word *Disciple.*"

Robert Chambers is a Church of God pastor, also from Michigan, and describes several changes they made to emphasize this more transformational dynamic of the Christian life.

We changed the name of "Sunday school" to "Christian Life Hour." We changed Wednesday night from "Prayer Meeting" to "Family Night," and the Sunday night service from our "Evangelistic Service" to our "Praise Service." And we started weekly "Discipleship Prayer Groups." This church had been in existence for 30 years and has had problems for most of those 30 years. There were six people attending when I became pastor thirteen years ago. We now have 234 members with over 200 in worship. My approach has been to break down the old molds and mindset, to introduce new methods, and to bathe all efforts in prayer. We also assign someone to personally disciple all new members. The members are taught that they are all ministers of God's Word.

The heart of the matter is that we are all ministers. When being a member means being a disciple, and being a disciple means being a minister, a very different ethos is created for a congregation than when members are seen as merely persons who have "joined" and then are asked to be "volunteers."

In a day when secular Americans, and especially younger generations, are not particularly attracted to institutional membership, the church must be very clear that to be "membered" to Christ is to be connected to all of his blessings and all of his sufferings for a world still needing to be reached with his love and gospel. Revitalized smaller churches are helping this old, old story be heard and sung as a new song, in part because they have learned to speak the language and interpret the meaning of "Christian Discipleship."

3. Employ Gifts for Ministry

Pastors leading small churches to new life and maturity are intentional about wanting to equip Christ's disciples for special ministries that match their gifts. Often this means knowing how to turn over to lay persons certain responsibilities that may have been initially carried by the pastor. Steve Drury, a Kentucky pastor, reports his goal is training people to be "pastors" not "lay people." Several men and women in his church have completed a Lay Speakers program and preach whenever he is absent. Steve Porter, a pastor in Louisiana, writes:

> Initially, I had to take charge in some unstable areas such as Youth Leader, Young Adult Sunday school class, Choir, Bible Study. I am no longer in charge of the Sunday school class nor the youth. Hopefully I will soon be able to relinquish control of the choir. This is a delicate matter. Sometimes people's feelings get hurt because they think they should be doing these things. But pay special attention to seeking people with gifts and talents who can do things. Get lay people more involved in the worship experience. Use them as lay readers, have them give the children's sermon, work to achieve a combination of young and old workers in the church. Let people work.

But emphasizing gifts for ministry is not only a matter of turning over jobs the pastor once did, it includes what Steve Porter describes above as "a delicate matter"—knowing how to match gifts with ministries, and how to include new people in positions of service and leadership. Pastor Fred Parklyn in Pennsylvania tells how he includes new members by making some "members at large" on the

122

Administrative Board and using as many as possible as "worship leaders." But he declares "IT'S NOT BEEN WITHOUT A STRUG-GLE!"

Although some pastors have tried with varying degrees of success to replace entrenched and uncooperative leaders—especially treasurers and musicians—with newer more flexible leaders, most try whenever possible to avoid such confrontations and emphasize instead creating new opportunities for new people. As the momentum shifts to accomplishing the new vision, new ideas and new possibilities emerge. The energy shifts away from the inflexible resisters. It is more beneficial to add opportunities for service and celebrate gifts, than to merely try to replace older leaders with new people. Eric Bell writes from Alabama:

> I try to enable people and let them have a part in ministry. I try to help them see what they can do that will help the church and the community. I try to make every job important, even sharpening pencils for the attendance registration pads. And I'm not coming up with all the ideas. They're coming from the congregation. That makes this a really fun place to be because there's always something to celebrate or enjoy. What I'm enjoying is finding the talents of people. It brings out stewardship of talents God has graced them with. They have made their own wooden table for the altar, created the stained glass insets for the doors, started two new children's choirs, put up a Christmas tree and invited the whole neighborhood to help decorate it, begun to share space and some worship with a Chinese congregation, and are talking of ways they can meet some of the needs of the students at the new elementary school being built next door.

It is important for all of us to feel needed and that we are contributing meaningfully to our common vision. Sometimes training is needed. Sometimes job descriptions have to be written. Sometimes all that is required is to get out of the way and let a person who knows how "just do it." But relationships are still more important than tasks alone. We need to do all that is possible to help everyone enjoy his or her fair share of contribution, based on God's guidance and the Spirit's gifts for ministry.

Rick Thornton, pastor of a wonderfully revitalized and growing church in Pennsylvania, believes that even persons on their way to Christ but not yet Christians, have gifts to give and can serve. This created a significant problem for the congregation to resolve. One unmarried couple who were living together began to attend the church. Before they had joined or publicly acknowledged their Christian faith, they were allowed to use their gifts and serve by standing at the door as greeters. One couple who had recently transferred into the church quoted scripture and "demanded" that this couple living in sin be removed from any and all positions of ministry. The matter was taken first to the elders and then to a counsel meeting. Both bodies affirmed that this was their congregational philosophy of ministry. Jesus loved the outcasts, the sinners, and the tax collectors and let them serve him. He still does, both before and after they know him as Savior and Lord. Nonchristians and nonmembers are restricted from certain roles in church leadership, but *every* person who wants to can do something!

The unmarried couple, without knowing of this turmoil, announced the next Sunday their decision to accept Christ and get married. They wanted the entire congregation to come to their wedding. There was great rejoicing at God's wondrous grace. In a four-page letter to the congregation Pastor Thornton affirmed his congregation and their understanding of both God's purpose and God's process. Part of the letter read:

> Though we know there is much sin in the world, somehow we are shocked when we see it in the lives of those in church. We long for a church that is made up of people who have their lives together and are no longer continuing in sin. The truth of the matter is that that has never been the case. The church does not depend on "pretty good people," the church depends on God's grace.
>
> All along the way, for the vilest sinner and the most obnoxious Christian sinner, God draws us to Himself. And He does it in little ways. He gives us little opportunities to respond and calls us to fuller commitment to Himself.
>
> Likewise, you at the Church of God at Yocumtown do "evangelism," inviting people to Jesus, in lots of little ways that take people from where they are and move them in a process towards all that God wants them to be. You encourage each "pre-Christian," those on the way to Jesus but not quite there, as well as each Christian to be in ministry. And before people know it, they have been swept up in God's plan for their lives. Yes, they reach a point where they know

and show their personal relationship with Christ but it comes at a point along the way.

If more pastors and churches could understand and practice this preconversion dynamic of God's grace, sometimes called prevenient grace, many more persons seeking God's touch on their lives would find it in our churches.

4. Encourage Small Groups

Many turnaround churches testify to the importance of small groups in the development of mature disciples. The book of Acts acknowledges that the early church knew the importance of meeting in homes as well as joining together for worship in the Temple (Acts 2:46). Most of the great redemptive movements throughout church history have discovered that long-lasting transformation requires the kind of community and accountability best experienced in small cells of four to twelve people. Currently some are even suggesting that the only true form of the church is a collection of cells.[7]

Sometimes members in small churches have felt little need for "small groups" since they say "We're not much more than that even when everyone is here." But the benefit of small groups is not so much to be found in their numbers as in their interactive and intentional agenda for Christian love, growth, service, and accountability. Small groups allow persons with different needs and interests to explore areas of personal growth and ministry without everyone needing to do so at the same time. Small groups are wonderful training labs for learning more about loving and caring for one another than is possible in the context of worship or in most Sunday school classes or Bible studies.

Barbara Florey, pastor of the Concord United Methodist Church in Michigan, says:

> Small groups are where I can be with people, and get to know them and have a really personal relationship with them. I'm very intuitive and I see people for what they can be and what they can do. I believe in them even long before they believe in themselves. Sometimes I'm wrong, and that's alright. I will lead the group the first time we go through something like The Workbook of Living Prayer, Disciple Bible Study, or Serendipity, always looking for people's strengths,

abilities, and gifts for ministry, and especially for potential leaders. The more we get people into these groups the more leaders emerge. The next time that short-term study is presented, I have one of them lead it. Then I have to shift my time priorities to spend more time working with these leaders and less time leading groups myself. It is wonderful to see people grow into the Christian leaders they are meant to be.

Small groups provide a safe and nurturing arena for the transforming work of the Holy Spirit. Gifts for ministry can be observed and encouraged by pastors and other church leaders.

But perhaps most important, here is where the part of the discipling process Jesus referred to as "teaching them to obey everything that I have commanded you" (Matt. 28:20) can best take place. In large groups, or teaching-talking-preaching kinds of groups, the obedience level is usually restricted to "oughts" and "shoulds." In small groups, five or ten persons can decide to do something, and hold one another accountable. Here people actually pray, bear one another's burdens, read the Bible, and report to one another week after week of what they are learning about being obedient to Christ. And although mission and outreach have already been discussed in the last chapter, small groups are often how persons become involved in this critically important aspect of Christian discipleship. Mission teams, visitation teams, and community ministry teams of all types are themselves usually small groups. Out of their study, prayers, and personal sharing, God leads them to act in joyful obedience, and they experience a whole new understanding of following Jesus. They will never be content again to simply say "Lord, Lord" for they have been changed from one degree of glory to another. More than likely they will be heard saying,

> "Lord, when was it that we saw you hungry and gave you food, or thirsty and gave you something to drink? And when was it that we saw you a stranger and welcomed you, or naked and gave you clothing? And when was it that we saw you sick or in prison and visited you?" And the king will answer them, "Truly I tell you, just as you did it to one of the least of these who are members of my family, you did it to me." (Matt. 25:37-40)

126

Disciples Imitate Leaders

The pastors who help bring transformation to smaller churches are themselves persons who believe deeply that God is able to change people and congregations from what they were and what they are to what they are yet to become. They are flexible in their leadership style according to the need, and they are committed to the transformation of others' lives, not just the advancement of their own plans and careers. They stimulate a vision of change through their example as well as their preaching and teaching, and they enable their congregations to clarify their specific purpose as well as plan specifically what they can do to make their dreams become reality.

They realize as well that changes in congregations depend on changes in individuals. Committed as they are to the great commission of Jesus to "make disciples," they help the congregation become more welcoming, more focused on stretching toward Christian maturity, more invested in using the gifts of every member and non-member, and more involved in small groups for nurture, accountability, and service.

Some of these pastors have had challenges beyond the normal array. They have been called not only to serve struggling churches, but also to serve in communities undergoing significant ethnic and cultural transitions. These pastors and their stories represent a unique slice of the missionary dimension of Christian ministry and read even more like New Testament Christianity than is the case with the colleagues. We turn now to the lessons of hope and power found in these special cases of churches in transitional communities.

VII

TURNING AROUND THE CHURCH IN TRANSITION

*Now during those days, when the disciples were in-
creasing in number, the Hellenists complained against
the Hebrews because their widows were being neglected in the daily distribution of food.*

Acts 6:1

*What are the barriers that separate persons? Are
they visible or invisible? Race, religion, education,
status? Consider how you can deal with this. Certainly, one function of the gospel is reconciliation.*[1]

Change

Persons, communities, and churches change. But change is dis-
ruptive, uncomfortable, and often resisted, especially by individuals
and institutions that have the most investment in the past and the
status quo. Yet change is at the heart of the gospel. The inbreaking

128

of the kingdom of God requires radical shifts in values and viewpoints.

Learning about these changes and adjusting to them has never been easy or automatic for God's people. Christian disciples through the ages have struggled to implement the command of Christ and the leading of Holy Spirit to "make disciples of all peoples." Why? Because Jews and Samaritans, Jews and Greeks, and "Hebrews and Hellenists" are different. Their basic needs are the same, but their values and viewpoints are not. They have been oriented to life through different cultures, and they find it difficult to feel "at home" with one another, even in the church. Nevertheless, the Spirit of God is always at work to reshape their differences into a larger mosaic of meaning more fully revealing the power and purpose of God in creating new communities of the kingdom.

This chapter looks at churches experiencing turnaround in communities undergoing ethnic and cultural change. What can we learn from these churches about how the kingdom comes? Are there any distinctive leadership qualities, emphases, or skills needed in such places? What are the approaches to outreach and evangelism that prove most effective? What can we learn from the scripture itself and from modern day studies in cross-cultural Christian ministry known as "missiology"?

Many churches in changing communities across this land are trying to learn the answers to questions like these. Their efforts at ministry produce results that are not always ideal, but neither were those we read about in the New Testament. The early church, even in the fresh pentecostal power of the Holy Spirit, struggled to become Christ's one Body composed of many diverse members. We see in Acts 6 that under pressure, "Hebrews" (conservative, Aramaic-speaking Jews who resisted adapting to the secular Greek society around them) and "Hellenists" (Jews who adjusted to Greek society, spoke its language, and probably came from outside of Jerusalem) didn't naturally relate well to each other.

And the story of the conflict and change continued as the gospel crossed over into the lives of Greeks who were not Jews at all. Peter, Paul, and the whole early church had to adjust again and again as God moved to establish new outposts of the kingdom and form one Body in Christ (Acts 10, Galatians 3:28). Arguments broke out, feelings were hurt, various perspectives had to be aired, prayer had

129

to be offered, and long hours of discussion had to take place (Acts 15). Even then, tensions over cultural practices and preferences made it difficult for the goals of the kingdom of God to be fully manifest all at once. The sometimes painfully slow process of cultural reorientation required constant attention and the gift of wisdom throughout Paul's ministry (Romans 14–15), and of course the same is true today.

In the context of this high calling and the challenge of ethnically changing communities, the following stories emerge as samples of modern day accounts of smaller churches faithfully offering the gospel and working out their own salvation.

Three Stories to Set the Stage

Trinity Church

The Reverend Linda Poteete-Marshall finished her seminary education in Boston and was appointed to the staff of the large downtown First Church in Santa Monica, California. Two years later, anxious to be pastor at her own church, she was appointed to a small congregation in southeastern Los Angeles County. For more than twenty years this once strong and flourishing congregation had been struggling for survival. On its one hundredth anniversary Sunday, just one month before Linda arrived, it rallied one hundred for worship; but the best it could do for her first Sunday service in July was thirty. Linda's friends felt she deserved "better" and told her it was a "horrible appointment."

The few remaining active members were mostly white "Anglos" in a changing neighborhood that was now 80 percent Hispanic. Some efforts had been made previously to reach the newer residents, but to little avail. There were significant differences in addition to the obvious language and cultural barriers. Many of the newer families in the neighborhood were undocumented immigrants from Mexico. Income for survival often came from illegal activities. Problems with drugs and violence had been on the increase. It appeared to many who had been watching this church and serving it through the years, that the future was dim, and perhaps it was time for letting go, closing down, and moving on.

Five years later, Trinity United Methodist Church and its pastor, Linda Poteete-Marshall, received from the denomination an evangelism award for churches with fewer than one hundred members.

130

In that year alone there had been a 54 percent increase in membership amounting to twenty-three new members, all part of the newer immigrant community. What happened? The Reverend Poteete-Marshall and her congregation had discovered how to claim their identity as Christ's presence in the world by bringing good news to the poor and breaking down the dividing walls between ethnic groups.

Church of All Nations

Wee-Li Tan grew up in a Christian family in Singapore. His grandfather was a Presbyterian minister in China before moving with his family to become a missionary in Singapore. At the age of eighteen, Wee-Li came to the realization that he needed a vital and personal relationship with Jesus Christ. This was a turning point in his life and led to his call to ministry. He pursued his theological studies in England and then worked for evangelistic organizations traveling throughout western Europe and Africa.

When the Reverend Tan was appointed to pastor the Church of All Nations, the average Sunday morning worship attendance was fifty-eight, most of whom were African American. Many cultural adjustments were ahead as this small congregation accepted their first Asian pastor. But this 125-year-old church had a long history of serving people in need without regard for their race or class. Nearly a hundred years earlier, under the leadership of the Reverend Edgar J. Helms, Morgan Chapel—as it was then called—became the birthplace of what is today known as Goodwill Industries. In 1917 Morgan Memorial Methodist Church first acquired the name "Church of All Nations" as it began holding worship in various languages (mostly European) to meet the needs of the changing neighborhood.

Changes continued through the decades. In 1963 the beautiful Gothic structure erected in 1917 was demolished to make room for the Massachusetts Turnpike. Goodwill Industries relocated to another section of the city and became separated from Morgan Memorial. In 1975 the present church facility was completed; but in the decade that followed, little of Morgan Memorial's "all nations" identity remained. The needs of the neighborhood and the newly arriving ethnic groups in the city continued to change, but Morgan Memorial had not been able to keep pace. The gifts and vision of the newly appointed pastor were about to make a difference. A heritage was about to be recovered.

131

Within four years after Pastor Tan's arrival, worship attendance had increased over 100 percent. Sunday school attendance was up 86 percent, and perhaps the most exciting transition to take place was the amazingly strong multiethnic nature of the emerging congregation. Today over thirty different nationalities and ethnic identities are represented in those who worship and serve through its various ministries. Persons from Barbados to Zimbabwe make this their church home and together have revealed for old downtown Boston a new vision of harmony and hope. In an age of racial prejudice and distrust, this church stands as a witness that the gospel of God's love in Jesus Christ is for all people.

First Church of God, York
     The Reverend Gil Livingston describes himself as truly converted to Christ at age forty-eight. He had been asked by his pastor to speak from the pulpit on Laity Sunday, and as he prepared his message he realized he could only be saved by God's wonderful and amazing grace through faith in Jesus Christ and not by working his way to heaven. He gave himself with a new spirit to witnessing and helping at church. He began to work with the church's youth program and built it from 15 to 106 in three years.
     As time passed he knew he was being called to give his remaining years to full-time ministry. He retired from his lifelong work as a railroad engineer and began his denomination's course of study for pastoral ministry. As his first pastoral task he agreed to serve a dying congregation in downtown York, which could not pay his salary. Ten years later, at age seventy, Gil and his wife are preparing themselves for retirement and the revitalized First Church of God, York, Pennsylvania for their new pastor.
     The neighborhood around this old First Church had significantly changed through the decades of the 1970s and 1980s. The ethnic makeup had shifted from its traditional, stable 98 percent blue collar and middle-class white population to a mosaic representing 21 percent African Americans, 5 percent Hispanic Americans, 1 percent Asian Americans, and 71 percent Euro-Americans (USA born). As the new suburbs developed and many moved out, the older parts of York declined in typical fashion leaving little sense of community and a growing number of social problems. Into this setting came the Reverend and Mrs. Gil Livingston to live

in the parsonage next to the church and begin their ministry in what the denomination called a "Revitalization Project."

Under the leadership of the conference church growth consultant, the Reverend James Moss, this project tried to enable several older and declining congregations to go through a three-year process of death and resurrection. In some cases the name of the church was even changed as efforts were made to celebrate and leave behind the old and bring to life an entirely new congregation. But the most important ingredient in the process was the development of a new constitution by a selected and representative council including the pastor who would come to lead the new church. York First Church has proven to be the most successful effort in this program.

When the revitalization project began the church was averaging twenty in one morning worship service and twenty-five in two Sunday school classes. Ten years later two morning worship services average 114 and twelve Sunday school classes average 70 in attendance. Ten years ago the only activities held were worship and Sunday school. Now, activities include: the Monday morning Bible Study for women, the Tuesday night Prayer and Bible Study, the Wednesday night JOY Bible Club for Children and Slim and Trim for women, the very successful Wednesday and Friday evening "Five F's" support program (Friends For Freedom From Fear), the Thursday night Basics of Christian Faith group, the Saturday morning men's breakfast once a month, and every other month, the women's meeting on Tuesday evenings. In addition, the church is engaged in a "Biblical Counseling" ministry, which offers private, personal counseling for "everyone and everything." Over $200,000 have been spent in ten years to repair and renovate the church facility and to buy property and apartment buildings next door in order to expand the church's ministries to the community. Gil Livingston has been wonderfully used by God to bring new life to a dying church in a changing community.

The Churches

Twenty percent of the small churches that we studied are experiencing noticeable ethnic and cultural shifts in their community. Two observations can be made about these churches.

First, as might be expected, small churches experiencing this kind of "transition" are more likely to exist in towns and cities than

133

in villages and rural areas. Forty-eight percent of the churches experiencing "little" or "no" change are in communities with populations of less than 2,500. In contrast, only 15 percent of the "transitional churches" are in similar sized communities.

Second, the transitional churches are slightly larger in membership (163 to 153) but smaller in average worship attendance (96 to 122) than the churches reporting little or no ethnic shift. But what is most interesting is the short time line of their growth. The transitional churches report membership growth of 91 percent over the last five years as compared to 48 percent for the churches in the more ethnically stable communities. Similarly, they report greater five-year increases in worship attendance (123 percent compared to 68 percent), Sunday school enrollment (140 percent compared to 99 percent), Sunday school attendance (47 percent versus 42 percent), and budget expenses (130 percent to 80 percent). Yet even with their more rapid growth, their functional congregations are smaller when measured by average worship attendance, and children and youth enrolled in church school.

It is not easy to say with any confidence why these transitional churches have experienced significantly more rapid growth when measured as percentage growth. Perhaps it is random variation in a relatively small sample. Perhaps it has something to do the population pool of unchurched neighbors in more urban contexts versus more rural contexts. Or perhaps it is just that the "transitional churches" identified for this study started their turnaround closer to survival numbers. Percentage growth gives the apparent advantage to the smaller initial group. Thus a church of twenty growing by twenty reveals a 100 percent increase. A church of fifty growing by twenty reveals only a 40 percent increase.

In any case, these churches and their pastors have shown that significant growth is possible and is happening in places often seen as difficult and challenging, if not "impossible."

Who Are the Pastors?

Although the turnaround pastors in the transitional churches are in many ways not much different from other pastors there are some telling variations.

1. Personal Backgrounds

These variations show up first in their personal backgrounds. First, they tend to be older by an average of five to six years. Second, women are more likely to be found serving these growing transitional churches than the other revitalized congregations in the study (28 percent compared to 9 percent). Third, they are more likely to be single and with no children living at home. Fourth, they were slightly older on average when they first became involved in church (9.1 years as compared to 7.8 years) as well as when they first experienced a time of deep commitment or conversion (20 years compared to 17). Fifth, although both groups report being from active church families, the pastors serving a transitional church are twice as likely to have experienced denominational shifts at some point in their lives (67 percent compared to 33 percent). Sixth, they are slightly more likely to have come from urban community backgrounds (61 percent compared to 54 percent). Seventh, they are almost twice as likely to report no cultural conflicts or adjustments encountered as they started their ministry in their churches (50 percent compared to 27 percent).

It is difficult to summarize all of the above. Most of the differences noted are slight. However, it might be said that "experience counts." The experience of age, the experience of having lived through change, and the experience of being a woman in American society may all help produce the qualities and confidence needed to lead struggling churches in changing communities into new life and effective ministries.

2. Professional Backgrounds

When it comes to their professional backgrounds and ministry perspectives, again they are very similar to their colleagues in more stable communities with three exceptions. First, they have a much more difficult time labeling themselves theologically. Significantly more chose a combination of theological labels that included "evangelical" (for example "evangelical/charismatic") than chose "evangelical" by itself, and they were almost four times as likely to claim the label "liberal" either by itself or in combination with other terms. Cross-cultural experience often changes us so that we no longer fit snugly into neatly defined camps. These pastors seem to have be-

135

come more comfortable with finding value in a variety of perspectives, and this may tell us why they are fit and not frustrated when serving in communities where diversity and change are standard fare.

Second, they were more likely than the other pastors in the sample to describe their evangelistic concern as "wanting others to personally know God" (22 percent as compared to 8 percent). These are evangelistic pastors and "evangelical" even if not simply "Evangelicals."

Third, they are less likely to have had evangelism classes in seminary (44 percent compared to 52 percent) and more likely to have had "much" training in evangelism prior to entering the ministry (22 percent compared to 6 percent).

Once again, it seems that "experience" is an important distinguishing characteristic of turnaround pastors in transitional communities. Because of their real life experience these pastors are not as comfortable with simplistic theological "labels." They define their evangelistic and ministry goals more in terms of experience— "knowing God." And finally, they learned more about evangelism from experience and more about ministry from practitioners than from professors.

Eight Emphases for Ministry

When trying to summarize the leadership and ministry characteristics that contribute to turnaround in transitional churches, eight special emphases emerge. We have seen them before; however, they take on added value and significance when viewed against the backdrop of their challenging context. Even more than their colleagues serving elsewhere, effective pastors facing the challenge of cultural change in their communities emphasize the following.

1. A Biblical Center

A generation or more of writers who have analyzed growing churches and the pastors who serve them have described their commitment to Scripture.[2] Turnaround pastors clearly confirm this priority, and those in transitional communities demonstrate an even greater dependence on Scripture than do their colleagues.

136

When asked what additional training or resources have been most helpful to their ministries, "the Bible" becomes their number one answer (ranked eighth by the rest of the sample). Favorite passages for informing their ministry were Matthew 28:18-20 (also number one for the rest of the sample) and Matthew 25 (ranked eighth by the rest of the sample)—an interesting balance of the great commission and "unto the least of these."

This group of pastors is also more likely to draw strength and shape their visions for ministry from the images of the prophets. Linda Poteete-Marshall didn't so much select her favorite passage as discover it as a vision experience.

> I guess I was just too naïve and new at the whole thing to even consider failure as an option. And I was pregnant with my first child. It was wonderful! Life was wonderful! Then one morning as I stood looking out the window on the backyard totally dead and brown because the sprinkling system had not been used in years, I had a vision—a sort of waking dream. I saw water being poured out on the brown grass. All the brownness was being transformed into fresh, green, new life. I had a special interest in Jeremiah while in seminary, and recalled the "new planting" image he used several times as God's vision for Israel and Judah.
>
> "I will set my eyes upon them for good, and I will bring them back to this land. I will build them up, and not tear them down; I will plant them, and not pluck them up. I will give them a heart to know that I am the LORD; and they shall be my people and I will be their God, for they shall return to me with their whole heart." (Jer. 24:6-7)
>
> "If you will only remain in this land, then I will build you up and not pull you down; I will plant you, and not pluck you up." (Jer. 42:10a)
>
> I was confident this was what God had in mind for us. I knew the greatest need was not money, but a new vision of what God wanted to do here for, with, and through these faithful few. And I was ready to begin.

The importance these pastors place on having a biblical center shows up in their answers to quite a variety of questions. When asked what suggestions they would offer to other pastors serving in similar situations, they recommended "teaching God's purpose from the Bible" as number five (ranked seventeenth by the others). Likewise when asked to offer recommendations to seminaries as they prepare pastors to serve smaller churches, they responded as their number one answer "relate the Bible to life" (ranked fifteenth by others). These are pastors who live in and from the Bible and are confident God will speak through its pages today to address the challenges they face in modern society.

2. A Heart for the Congregation

Sometimes struggling churches in changing neighborhoods are afraid that their new pastors will blame them for the problems they face, or try to change them but without understanding their grief and pain. Sometimes denominational leaders are seen as outsiders who will push the new pastors to "bite the bullet," overcome congregational resistance, and make the hard choices come what may. When these perceptions are based on reality, the usual result is failure, and thus one more reason for congregations to wonder whose side their judicatory leaders, and even their pastors, are on.

The pastors serving in changing communities are more likely to overcome obstacles by "loving and understanding the congregation" (ranked fourth as compared to twelfth by their colleagues). It may well be that the intentional effort of loving the remnant members becomes even more important for congregational renewal in times of ethnic and cultural shift.

The pastor of a church facing ethnic shift in Big Lake, Texas, writes "I wanted them to know that I understood their way of life (oil fields and ranching) and did not wish to change tradition. What happened in the past we can do nothing about, but you can love your neighbor as yourself." He adds, "We virtually started over, and the congregation began to work when they understood that I came to stay as long as God needed me and that I loved each of them, warts and all."

Another pastor from a small town in Kansas writes "My twenty-eight years as a teacher and coach have developed my people skills. I always try to meet people where they are in their spiritual walk. I try to let them know that I do love and care for them."

The United Methodist Church in Notasulga, Alabama experienced an additional dimension to their pastor's love for the congregation. The following appears in the church's historical report prepared for its 155th anniversary year.

138

In 1986, our present pastor began to challenge the church and our community with the statements: "God loves you just like you are, but He loves you too much to leave you like you are" and "The best and greatest days are before you, not behind you." The church responded and the community was impacted.

Loving and being loved is not an end in itself, but rather an indispensable and divinely appointed means for a congregation to hear the voice of God call them toward loving their neighbors.

3. Compassion for the Community

The pastors in these transitional communities were not only lovingly supportive of their congregations, they also had a missionary mindset toward the persons of the community. When they describe their efforts to contact persons in the community, they rank "pastoral care extended to the community" third, while their colleagues rank it seventeenth. These men and women are leading their congregations toward change and turnaround by initiating loving, personal contact with neighbors who are often seen as persons outside the comfort zone, persons who are different.

Jesus spent a great deal of time helping his disciples understand how to cross these cultural barriers.[3] Pastors who successfully lead their churches to new life across the boundaries often established by culture and reinforced by sin, are more likely than their colleagues to have had cross-cultural experience and valued it. Sometimes this experience is gained by living in a land other than one's own. Sometimes it is derived from giving serious study to a "foreign" language or philosophy or theology. Sometimes it comes by being a "minority" within one's own land or by experiencing life in two or more regions of the country. Southern California, Michigan, Alabama, and Maine offer plenty of opportunity for cultural diversity and experiencing something of the "us" and "them" mentality.

Because more and more of America is becoming multiethnic, pluralistic, and heterocultural, training and experience in cross-cultural communication and ministry is critical for the effective "mission" pastor and church leaders of today and tomorrow. One major mainline denomination recently completed a study of its smaller congregations and concluded among other things that pas-

139

toral assignments needed to be "intentionally made to the community as well as to the congregation in order to provide ministry appropriate to specific rural, urban, racial/ethnic, economic, and culturally diverse contexts."[4] The challenge is how to find and/or train those needed for this task.

Multitudes of lay persons and pastors are being positively influenced by short-term mission programs whether they stay in their own communities and join a Habitat for Humanity project, or travel to foreign lands. Volunteerism in many forms is on the increase as the baby boomers arrive at the stage in life where they want to contribute something to others.[5] Many change agents in communities and congregations will be drawn from this age group. They will be best equipped for this task in multiethnic, multicultural contexts if they already have expanded their own horizons through meaningful and reflective experience in cross-cultural ministry.

Likewise, we need to see how much help there is in the Bible as it addresses these very concerns. The passage that began this chapter is from Acts 6:1-7 and is an ideal model for at least part of the cross-cultural issue facing the church today even as it did in A.D. 33. "Hebrews" (Jewish old-liners and purists who spoke Hebrew) and "Hellenists" (Jewish newcomers who spoke Greek and arrived from other lands) didn't naturally "share" when it came right down to it, and "old-liners" and "newcomers" often still don't. Leaders must pay attention to the murmurings of the "new folk" and devise a plan that seems good to all. Quite a challenge.

Notice the apostles kept the ministry of prayer and outreach evangelism ("serving the word") as the priority even though equity problems developed along cultural lines as their fellowship expanded. In addition, the apostles opened wide the doors of shared leadership in solving the problems of the new kingdom community, reminding the members that being "full of the Spirit and wisdom" were the only true qualifications for being selected. Those selected were all Hellenists, and were publicly consecrated and supported in prayer.

Jesus was fond of reminding his listeners that they needed new ears and eyes to discern the kingdom. Leaders in churches having cross-cultural opportunities and challenges surely need to be full of the Spirit and wisdom, and they also need to know how to "see and hear" beyond the restrictions of monocultural experience. This leads naturally to another characteristic of leadership found in the twenty pastors studied who were serving churches in transitional communities.

4. A Listening Ear

Listening that uses one's full attention and produces an appropriate response, communicates respect and demonstrates love as well or better than any other single human activity. Cartoons in the newspapers are frequently developed around the tension produced when the husband, wife, friend, employee, or neighbor fails to pay attention to the one speaking. These cartoons strike us as humorous because they remind us of events we ourselves experience frequently. I am not sure about your refrigerator, but ours is covered with cartoons clipped and torn from newspapers because someone in the family wants to "say" something to someone else. Strange how many of the cartoons on our magnetic bulletin board depict a husband or father.

Listening is hard work; important hard work. Turnaround pastors in changing communities are good listeners. All pastors were asked to describe population, ethnic, and other demographic changes in their communities. The pastors in transitional communities were significantly less likely to have "estimated" their answers (17 percent compared to 35 percent) and more likely to have secured "hard data" through census reports, CIDS,[6] denominational studies, or other published data (72 percent compared to 47 percent). They realize the importance of working from good information.

At the same time, they were not merely content to read reports prepared by others. When asked if they or their congregations had made intentional efforts to gather information on their communities, 67 percent responded affirmatively. The Reverend Livingston in York, Pennsylvania, collected information from the city planning office, from telephone surveys using the city directory, and from door-to-door visitation. The Reverend Poteete-Marshall in Los Angeles County secured assistance from two different Spanish-speaking seminary students and went door to door to determine how the church could be more helpful in addressing the needs of the community. Love begins with listening and then does something about what is heard.

141

5. A Commitment to Prayer

Perhaps loving and listening to others and loving and listening to God are closely related skills or emphases. In any case, effective pastors in changing communities emphasize both an openness toward the community and an openness toward God in prayer.

Prayer is an activity all of us feel most drawn to during times of stress and when we feel inadequate to the challenge before us. As a pastor of a small church in a culturally mixed neighborhood experiencing a high crime rate especially among juveniles, this writer found himself frequently on his knees. A sense of helplessness and "being in over our heads" often encourages a spirit of prayer. Pastors and congregations in such challenging settings are well aware that "unless the LORD builds the house, those who build it labor in vain" (Ps. 127:1). Prayer for a sense of God's presence, guidance, blessing, and power seems only natural, and reminds everyone in the church and in the community, whose work this really is.

The Reverend Jeff Dunn in Bennettsville, South Carolina, simply writes: "We have no doubt that the only reason for what has happened is that God has graciously answered our prayers. In fact, God has done 'immeasurably more' than all we could have asked or imagined."

When describing the factors most important for their growth, the pastors in these challenging communities rated prayer as number six, seven positions above those serving more stable communities. When offering suggestions to other pastors, prayer is their number one recommendation. When describing their leadership role in the congregation, they frequently mention modeling and leading in prayer. They not only pray themselves, but also lead their congregations into new intimacy with God and a sense of divine empowerment through emphasizing prayer circles, prayer partners, prayer chains, prayer groups, prayer times in worship, and prayer ministries. Such an emphasis declares openly that these congregations trust in God and care about the needs of all people.

6. A Passion for Worship and Preaching

As in any effective Christian congregation, Sunday worship is the most important event in the weekly life cycle. More than any other single factor, alive and culturally appropriate worship is what holds these congregations together. Without intentional efforts to produce this kind of worship experience, churches may end up expanding their mission efforts in the community without incorporating any new members into the spiritual life of the congregation. When this happens, both the congregation and the community lose.

Perhaps no other writer at the end of the twentieth century has addressed the meaning of mission with more breadth and depth than David Bosch, who served as professor and head of the department of missiology at the University of South Africa until his untimely death in 1991. In his final work, *Transforming Mission: Paradigm Shifts in Theology of Mission*, Bosch lists five critical factors for a congregation's success in accomplishing its missionary task.

> The missionary dimension of a local church's life manifests itself, among other ways, when it is truly a worshipping community; it is able to welcome outsiders and make them feel at home; it is a church in which the pastor does not have the monopoly and the members are not merely objects of pastoral care, its members are equipped for their calling in society; it is structurally pliable and innovative; and it does not defend the privileges of a select group.[7]

It is the task of the pastor and congregation as a "truly worshipping community" to "welcome outsiders and make them feel at home." But this is not accomplished merely by a friendly word and handshake. The church must be able to convince all who come that it is "pliable and innovative; and it does not defend the privileges (preferences, traditions, rituals, habits, and tastes) of a select group." To bring new people with different values and even "tastes" into a worshipful experience of the presence of the Lord, requires that new people find a pastor and congregation ready to "listen" to their heart needs as well as their social needs.

The pastors of turnaround churches in changing communities are sensitive and skilled preachers and worship leaders. They know by past experience and/or intuition that new persons need to feel "at home" in the worship experience. They employ the musical and artistic gifts of any possessing them to enable all to praise God with a "new song." They explain the old traditions and introduce some new ones representative of the new community. They learn and use songs and expressions in other languages when appropriate as a sign of being sensitive to all persons. They work to find and use illustrations in their preaching that relate to the issues and problems being faced by a variety of people. Above all, they pray for guidance and the presence of the Holy Spirit as they preach the gospel and offer a renewed vision of God's love and purpose for all persons.

The Reverend S. Rene McKenzie describes how the Boca Grande United Methodist Church in Florida was able to grow from thirty active participants to over two hundred (many of whom are only part-time residents) through "hard work on preaching" and a loving, informal, personal time of worship. She writes:

> One of the crucial aspects to our changed vision has been personal concern and a sense of intimacy, even during the sermon. They never know when a sermon will be congregational-participation time. They know it is our mission to care for people and to take on praying for strangers if they are loved by even one of our own. They know after ten minutes that this is not a place to stand on ceremony, but to stand on a personal faith and to reach out to others.

The Reverend Linda Poteete-Marshall used her five years of Spanish language studies as well as her visionary biblical preaching to help her transitional church in Los Angeles County, California address the spiritual needs of new worshipers in culturally relevant ways. She also employed the gifts and training of Myriam Escorcia, an experienced Nicaraguan Assemblies of God pastor, as well as wife and mother, who was studying for the ministry at a nearby seminary. Together they modeled the unity and diversity needed to bridge the gaps and provide hope and momentum for the vision of a revitalized spiritual home for the new people in the neighborhood.

The Reverend Wee-Li Tan, pastor of the Church of All Nations in Boston, reports his own strongest gifts as "preaching and teaching" and "worship enablement." He believes the most important factors enabling small churches to become renewed for ministry are "vital, meaningful worship centering around biblical preaching that is relevant to daily living" and "a warm friendly community life that welcomes newcomers in an intentional way." He adds:

> Besides the exciting/innovative worship, practical preaching and the development of a caring, loving community life (koinonia), the other

144

major reason we have grown has been our intentional efforts to develop a multi-ethnic congregation reflecting what Christ's Church is supposed to be (Revelation 5 and 7). The vision of a community where God has broken down the walls of racial prejudice and class/social distinctions, can be a reality in a small way here in our congregation where we have people from over twenty-five different nationalities. There is real integration here. In the context of the Church in the USA today where by and large congregations are segregated racially and by class, and where society is so divided, a community that embodies the gospel in this way is very attractive.

Frankly, not every pastor or congregation is going to be successful at this kind of cross-cultural, multiethnic effort. Many vital congregations in changing communities respect and cooperate with one another while maintaining a more homogeneous worshiping congregation. In fact, some of the churches in our study explored and even made efforts to merge diverse congregations without "success." The Linda Vista Presbyterian Church in San Diego was informed by the Presbytery that it would have to merge with a Korean congregation or be closed. The Reverend Richard Hayward writes: "The two churches were combined. The results were disastrous. After four years we were separated and both churches began growing."

Nevertheless, the pastors in these churches take their context seriously and place biblical preaching and vital worship at the forefront of their efforts to address the deepest needs of their worshiping congregations. Their goal is not so much to create an ideal church as it is to meet the needs of all they can with the gifts of all who are available.

7. A Total Community Team Ministry

This leads naturally to a seventh emphasis. Like the other pastors studied, those in changing communities are committed to developing lay leadership and being involved in a team ministry. However, their approach to team ministry includes not only using the gifts and skills of those in the congregation, but also creatively involving others recruited from the larger community. Perhaps this is a natural preference, or perhaps it is a necessity brought on by the demands of ministry in such settings.[8]

As we have already seen, these pastors try to secure the best information available about their communities. Likewise, they seek the best available resources and personnel to address the needs discovered. Social service agencies, community action organizations, schools, denominational leaders and agencies, other churches, as well as members of the congregation with special interests, experience, or training are all called on to help. In addition to using those already qualified, these pastors make sure others are being trained to fill the slots needed for new ministries.

One of the best examples of this whole process is in the story of Trinity United Methodist Church in Los Angeles County California and its pastor, Linda Poteete-Marshall. After listening in prayer and receiving a vision of God's intended blessing for the dying church, after receiving the congregation's vote to begin a Spanish language ministry, and after listening to the community by conducting a door-to-door survey of needs, this church began to address the social and spiritual needs of the community.

Linda offered a class in English. Thirty-five men and women were in attendance. A second round of classes attracted sixty. A third effort produced one hundred. A full-blown ministry was developing. The State Department of Education was contacted and a grant of $28,000 was secured to run the program and pay for rent. Adult and youth work teams from various churches in the area began to pitch in and help bring one transformation after another to the run-down rooms and grounds of the church.

Linda realized, however, that her struggling efforts at Spanish were not going to be adequate to truly touch the hearts and homes of her neighbors. Her first effort to use a young seminary student hadn't worked out. So she tried again and was led to Myriam Escorcia. Myriam immediately began a door-to-door ministry of witness, conversation, and invitation to home Bible studies. Later, after other churches agreed to pay half of Myriam's salary for one year, she began a weekly 9:00 A.M. Spanish language worship service in addition to her Friday night Bible study.

At first only fifteen or so showed up. The monthly offerings amounted to no more than sixty dollars. But as the months went by, the numbers increased. Thirty to forty persons were regularly in attendance, and others were showing much more interest after becoming involved in the English classes.

A sense of momentum was being experienced. A staff of ten were offering classes for preliterate, beginning, and intermediate English students. Classes were held both mornings and evenings, four days a week, and child care and children's programs were available at all times. Myriam's regular visiting in the neighborhood and her home Bible studies were reaching the neighborhood with the gospel. A new model for vacation Bible school was developed in the summer. A six-week summer camp was created for children in grades 4-8 that combined VBS curriculum, peace-making skills and field trips. Eighteen children attended. A Saturday night youth program was begun, and soon up to twenty-five young people were involved.

During Linda's fourth and fifth years Trinity United Methodist was chosen by the District as a special mission project. Urban Society funds were made available for heating and electrical work. Ten churches and 120 persons were coming and going almost continually to help with carpentry, painting, new floors, planting, and even totally replacing the old sprinkler system. Water was once again bringing the beauty of new life to old dry ground. Green grass, lovely flowers and trees began to appear. A women's group was begun and Myriam started teaching a class on Methodism. Sewing classes, training in computers, and piano and guitar lessons were offered.

The good news continued to be extended to the neighborhood. Twelve thousand flyers and door-hangers were distributed announcing the English classes, the special summer programs, the ten home Bible studies and the worship services. Myriam began a special program to train leaders for the home Bible studies. A full-time secretary was hired to help with all the telephone and paperwork generated by the successful new projects and programs Trinity United Methodist Church had generated. Over two hundred persons were now involved every week in the English classes. The Bishop's Round Table purchased a new van to help provide needed transportation for Sunday worship attendance, and plans were underway for a new program in family counseling. The vision of the Lord's water being poured out on Trinity's parched ground was emerging as a true prophetic reality. An older member of the congregation at Trinity United Methodist Church noticed another small but amazing change after their five years of successful ministry to the changing neighborhood—no graffiti had been written on the church for five years.

Pastor Linda Poteete-Marshall was in one sense working herself

147

right out of a job. She drew on every available resource to address every available need. Persons with skills and gifts and experience, both inside and outside of the congregation, were contacted and used. Others were discovered as they emerged through the new ministries. Training was provided to equip others to give leadership in multiple areas of ministry. This is the kind of total community team work needed in these special contexts of changing communities.

8. A Community-Based Evangelism

When the risen Lord called his eleven disciples together on the hillside in Galilee and gave them his final commission (Matt. 28:16-20), he instructed them to "go and make disciples." Many churches find their most fruitful approach to evangelizing is through invitation rather than extension. They utilize the kinship and friendship networks of their members and invite people to join them for worship. As these new visitors feel warmly welcomed and touched by the worship and the preaching, they respond with faith and commitment.[9]

Although this method is also employed by the churches in changing communities, it appears that their most effective means of reaching new disciples for Christ is through new programs of outreach that address their felt needs. These programs are aimed at multiple levels of human need—physical, social, spiritual—that are addressed simultaneously or at least sequentially. Evangelistic home Bible studies are carried on at the same time that food pantries, Twelve Step programs, and meetings with the school board are underway. In fact, much like the early church depicted in Acts 6:1-7, someone needs to keep on with "prayer and serving the word" while others address the needs of those neglected and "wait on tables."

It is keeping all this balanced and moving that presents special challenges and requires special skills from the pastoral leaders. The pastors in these churches are more likely to prioritize and recommend the need to "risk new ideas and programs"[10] as critical to effective evangelism and revitalization. These men and women also rank "time management" as the number three obstacle they face in leading their churches to new life and growth. Their counterparts in the culturally more stable communities mentioned this problem only once. Perhaps this is also why these pastors in transitional communities are more likely to lead their congregations to create and adopt formal mission statements (67 percent versus 52 percent). Without this kind of guidance for prioritizing their energies and resources, these pastors and their leadership team would soon be exhausted.

A great variety of challenges seem to cry out like sirens luring captains and their ships toward the rocks. They seem to have discovered that the way to care for their community while at the same time remaining faithful to the great commission means to make disciples as they go. Evangelism in revitalized smaller churches in transitional communities is aimed more at contacting the people "out there" than it is at inviting persons "in here." Both are at work; but new people in changing communities need to be convinced they are valued for who they are, where they are, before they feel truly wanted and welcomed at worship. Effective evangelism in these churches takes the "go" of Jesus' great commission very seriously.

Trinity United Methodist Church has been effective in fulfilling its rally cry "A lighthouse for the neighborhood!" Over the course of five years Linda's vision of a "replanting" like the one Jeremiah promised, has come to pass. But as the transformation was completed, the Reverend Poteete-Marshall held out to the congregation the words of another Old Testament prophet.

"I will bring you to Zion, my sacred hill, give you joy in my house of prayer, and accept the sacrifices you offer on my altar. My Temple will be called a house of prayer for the people of all nations." The Sovereign LORD, who has brought his people Israel home from exile, has promised that he will bring still other people to join them. (Isa. 56:6-8 GNB)

All of us are "exiles" brought by God's grace to Zion. May our sacrifices be acceptable to the Lord of all nations, and may we be engaged as commissioned by our Savior in bringing good news to all peoples. May those whose stories have been shared in these pages enable us all to be more profitable stewards of the gospel as we work and wait for the Sovereign Lord to bring still other people to join us in the family of God.

APPENDIX A
Preparing Turnaround
Pastors

Some observers argue that the era of the small church is past and that the future belongs to megachurches like those that have emerged during the last twenty-five years. It probably goes without saying that this new phenomenon of campus-churches with tens and even hundreds of thousands of members and worshipers is a significant and profound change. But to ignore the 350,000 or more existing congregations in North America (not to mention the rest of the world) that average fewer than one hundred in worship would be a mistake. These churches and the pastors who serve them represent an enormously significant network of Christian influence. The real question is how can more of these existing and tenacious smaller congregations be enlisted in a "Turnaround Movement" like that examined in the previous chapters.

The answer, of course, is not simple, but the evidence suggests that pastors make a lion's share of the difference. The question then becomes how to locate, enlist, equip, and encourage a growing cadre of such empowered pastoral leaders. As one who has pastored churches, served as a denominational program and field representative, and is now teaching in a seminary, I have reason to be concerned about how well we are doing this task. I would lend my voice to that of James Cushman, a Presbyterian Church USA spokesperson for the small church, who writes: "There is a tremendous need for training tenured seminary faculty members and . . . [denominational] officials in understanding the character and dynamics of small membership churches and the type of clergy leadership needed."[1]

Throughout much of this book we have acknowledged the importance of listening to the voices and needs of those we seek to influence. Thus, the primary thrust of the pages that follow is to provide a feedback loop for the voices of one hundred "turnaround experts" from smaller churches as they share their own ideas and experiences with two important groups—theological faculties and denominational leaders.

Evaluating Theological Education

James writes: "Not many of you should become teachers, my brothers and sisters, for you know that we who teach will be judged with greater strictness" (3:1). This is a sobering reminder of the weighty responsibility laid on the shoulders of those who serve Christ and his church as teachers. Sometimes as teachers we mistakenly believe our task is to teach "subjects"—meaning courses related to a body of knowledge. In reality, our calling is to teach "subjects"—meaning persons called of God to serve the church and the world. Therefore, it is entirely appropriate to listen carefully to the evaluations offered by some of these subjects regarding their preparation for serving Christ in smaller churches.

Not all of the participating pastors were formally trained at either Bible colleges or seminaries. Ten percent have only a high school education. Another 9 percent have some college but no degree. Six percent indicate they have no formal theological education, 13 percent have "some," and another 13 percent say they have completed a special denominational course of study designed for second career pastors. Three percent have M.A. degrees in theological education and 64 percent have completed the M.Div. degree. Forty-one seminaries and theological schools were listed as contributing at least in part to the theological education of these pastors.

APPENDIX A

The Most Helpful and Most Needed Courses

Since this study was especially concerned with learning more about smaller churches that are effective in evangelistic outreach and church growth, the pastors were asked to rank up to three courses in their academic work that best prepared them for work in evangelism. The top five subject areas and their weighted scores[2] appear below.

Courses Most Helpful for Effective Evangelism
1. Basic Evangelism (88)
2. New Testament Studies (35)
3. Preaching and Worship (32)
4. Field Work or CPE (24)
5. Church History or Biographies (20)

Although thirty-four areas of study were reported as helpful, these pastors overwhelmingly indicate they benefited most from a course in evangelism.

In addition, pastors were asked to rank the areas of study they wished had been emphasized more in their ministerial education. Their top five weighted answers to this inquiry likewise appear below.

Ministry Areas Needing More Attention
1. Basic Evangelism (46)
2. Personal Evangelism (31)
3. Counseling (27)
4. Church Growth (27)
5. Biblical Studies (26)

Additional scores include: Leadership and Administration (26), Homiletics and Biblical Preaching (24), Practical Programming (21), Spiritual Life, Prayer and Healing (21), Small Churches and Small Towns (14), Evangelistic Preaching (12), Conflict Management (12), Worship and Liturgy (11), Change Agent of Institutional Dynamics (11), and Pastoral Care (10). Although the scores are closer, again these pastors affirm the need for courses in evangelism and church growth (combined score of 116).

APPENDIX A

Recommendations for Seminaries

In a related but more general question, the pastors were asked what recommendations they would make to seminaries preparing pastors for ministry in smaller churches. Their answers are listed below in order of frequency.

1. Teach small membership church realities.
2. Teach church growth for small churches.
3. Provide more contact with effective pastors.
4. Require more preparation in biblical preaching.
5. Teach more about situational leadership.
6. Teach about prayer for the pastor and congregation.
7. Focus on the practical "how to's."
8. Prepare us to work with volunteers.
9. Offer more evangelism training.
10. Relate the Bible to life.
11. Teach more administration, finances, and management.
12. Help create the new vision needed by churches.

What would happen if seminaries committed to producing the finest pastors for the largest number of churches (those with under two hundred members) listened to the advice and encouragement of their most effective graduates who serve these churches? How could this "marketing research" change the way teachers and administrators design ministry education?

Listening to the "Experts"

One way of utilizing the lists cited above is to review a few of the actual comments offered by the pastors.

One young woman who studied at a seminary that did not offer an evangelism course, and who is serving her first church simply pleaded, "Please teach a course on Evangelism!" Another frustrated pastor said simply and directly: "The weakest area in our seminaries is evangelistic studies. You cannot teach what you have not defined, and I am not sure they know what evangelism is." Several requests were made for more of the basics "like how to win someone to Jesus Christ, how to preach for a decision and be

154

biblical, and how to help new and older Christians develop to maturity."

Many feel that more experience in preaching is needed, and several report that they graduated from seminary having preached only one public sermon. Others express concern that they were not trained in "biblical preaching." One person commented, "Teach them first and foremost to teach and preach the Bible—almost anything and anyone will be accepted if his or her ideas are biblically based."

In addition, several made comments like, "We need more than just preaching skills, we need communication skills. Teach us how to deal with the different personalities and ages of church members, how to work with large and small congregations, and how to establish new ministries." Some also focused on the importance of listening skills. One pastor said, "Pastors need to know how to build rapport and trust relationships with their people. They need to learn how to ask their people what their vision is for growth and what witness for Christ they want to have in the community, and then know how to guide them toward that vision."

Another area needing attention is learning how to relate to the ministry context. One said, "Teach them how to be positive in their attitude toward small churches and that small churches are made up of God's people too." A retired Army chaplain added, "We were trained to serve large churches and be professional. The opposite should be taught and practiced." Many called for more "study of the sociological factors involved in ministry and the nature of the small town family." A common concern was the feeling of being totally unprepared to deal with the values, attitudes and actions of pagan children, youth and adults. Several recounted how they were helped by studies in cultural anthropology, sociology, contextual theology, and even "missiology."

Actually, much of what these pastors are asking for could be listed under the heading "Practical How To's" such as how to: (1) manage conflict, (2) handle finances and stewardship, (3) serve as a pastoral change agent, (4) nurture brand new believers, (5) help persons discover and use their gifts for ministry, and (6) pray as we ought.

It should be obvious that turnaround pastors are not merely asking for more courses in evangelism and church growth—

although this clearly is their number one suggestion. These pastors are facing secular ideas and values both in the church and in the world and they need biblical studies and spiritual disciplines that equip them for today's challenges and opportunities. They face a world full of growing violence, abuse, divorce, and confusion and ask for better skills to know how to counsel and guide those who are hurting. Most sense they were unprepared for the conflict and power struggles they encountered as they tried to lead their congregations through change. Unless they had a background in business, nearly all these hard-working and naturally gifted leaders sensed a need for more training in administration, finances, serving as a change agent, and practical programming.

It might be argued that no academic curriculum can adequately prepare pastors in all areas, and that some things are better learned through continuing education events after pastors are in the field. Nevertheless, the most successful pastors are calling for additional preparation in the areas listed above while in seminary, not after they leave. How well are we listening to their voices? How would the shape of theological education change if we did?

These are days of reevaluating the meaning of theological education for more than just mainline seminaries. The Association of Theological Schools, which sets the accrediting standards for theological education in North America, is engaged in seeking answers to the question, "What is good theological education?" Daniel Aleshire writes:

> The question invites schools to think about the ways in which their tasks change as the student bodies they educate change. It also invites questions about the kind of leadership that may be most needed in North American churches, parishes, and religious communities. Is it the kind of leadership that has been available in the past, or does the changing social location of religion itself require new images of the qualities most desired in religious leaders? As professional schools, theological schools are intrinsically concerned with the character of leadership.[3]

Preparing leaders has not been the only or even the primary goal of theological education in the past. Perhaps that is why some have preferred to use terms like "ministerial education" or "seminary education" to describe a larger agenda than the study of theology. But even as the Association of Theological Schools acknowledges that a new day has come that demands leaders who are "able to nurture and revitalize ailing institutions by helping them to develop new visions for ministry and rediscover their theological identities,"[4] no mention is made of "outreach evangelism" in the lists of needed leadership skills and responsibilities. Is there a blind spot? Can the church of Jesus Christ fulfill its calling in this age and neglect training pastors for their role in the apostolic ministry of the gospel?

The Importance of Mentors

Whatever the next generation's church leaders will receive as their tools for ministry, one thing is certain: people who effectively lead small churches will still learn much of what they know from the persons who teach them. What can today's effective pastors of small churches teach us as they describe the qualities most valued in their mentors?

"What mentor or teacher has contributed most to your effective pastoral ministry? Why or how?" Pastors were asked these questions primarily to discover which professors most influenced successful small church pastors. However, as sometimes happens, much more was learned than was expected. Well over half of the most helpful "teachers" of pastors are themselves pastors, and not professors. Although no way exists to determine which of the professors mentioned might likewise qualify as experienced pastors, it is obvious that working or having worked as a pastor is an important asset when mentoring those who are interested in becoming pastors. One pastor summed it up this way in describing his professor-mentor: "He is an excellent teacher, knows the parish, has been a pastor, has strong personal faith and commitment to Christ, and understands the average lay person."

Mentors, by definition, are wise and trusted counselors. Turn-around pastors indicate that their contact with persons of faith, character, knowledge, experience, vital piety, love, and human compassion was critically important to inspiring and modeling their own ministries. Perhaps one of the most important questions that needs to be asked of every professor, pastor, and denominational leader is, "Who are you currently mentoring?" Jesus taught the multitudes, he mentored his disciples.

It may not always be easy to know how valuable we are to those we seek to influence for effective service in God's kingdom. But it *is* obvious that successful church leaders are most influenced by teachers and pastoral models who care about them and about the impact of the gospel. It is the combination that makes the difference. Perhaps this is what Paul was saying when he wrote:

> Though we might have made demands as apostles of Christ . . . we were gentle among you, like a nurse tenderly caring for her own children. So deeply do we care for you that we are determined to share with you not only the gospel of God but also our own selves, because you have become very dear to us. . . . As you know, we dealt with each one of you like a father with his children, urging and encouraging you and pleading that you lead a life worthy of God, who calls you into his own kingdom and glory. (1 Thess. 2:7-8, 11-12)

Partnerships for Theological Education

In the last decade of this century pastors of some of the largest churches have begun to select and mentor their staff associates out of their own congregations. They are helping, along with others, to raise the question whether seminaries can produce in isolation from the local church the kinds of persons needed to lead the most significant churches of tomorrow. According to the responses of pastors of smaller churches, this is not simply a question for the megachurches. Several suggested that seminaries ought to "partner" with some excellent pastors serving small churches and arrange for more firsthand internship experiences.

The Church of All Nations in Boston, pastored by Wan-Li Tan, is one of the "small churches" in our study. This congregation is now a "Training Parish" for seminarians and has five or more interns assigned there for up to a year. In addition, usually as many as fifteen seminarians from local schools worship with them regularly. In the last few years, five members of their church have become certified candidates for ordained ministry and are beginning their own theological studies as well as remaining active in their home church.

If seminaries would seek from among their graduates and other like-minded pastors a list of the finest mentors and models of effective ministry in the area, including those in smaller churches and cluster arrangements, to establish a network that identifies how best to utilize interns, the present gap between seminary education and congregational reality could be significantly reduced. Theological education in the twenty-first century will need to be much more congregationally based than has been the case during the last one hundred years.

Heeding the advice offered in the list of recommendations to seminaries ("Provide more contact with effective pastors") I arranged to have three of the pastors who participated in the study and their spouses speak to a class I was teaching on evangelism in the small church. The students were captivated by their presentations. One was even brave enough to say to my face, "The best thing about my whole seminary education was hearing her speak." What could I say? And best of all the pastors were thrilled to be asked! Everyone benefited.

The Role of Denominations

Much of the discussion above about enhancing the relationship between local churches and seminaries could be repeated when talking about denominations and their program and field staffs. Leadership networks and interdenominational training programs and resources have exploded over the last three decades, and show no sign of diminishing in influence. Much of the program assistance pastors previously sought almost exclusively through their denominational headquarters can now be secured through multiple other sources. Flyers for training programs, manuals, videos, consultants, periodicals, specialized newsletters, and "congresses" of all types are piled high on every pastor's desk. Furthermore, most denominations would be hard-pressed to offer the same quality in leadership or resources that is available through these networks and independent organizations.

What then is the role of denominational leaders in the days ahead, especially in relationship to the multitude of smaller churches they are responsible for? Four possible priorities emerge from the pastor survey: (1) become senior mentors to promising junior pastors, (2) creatively monitor and provide some special funding to help selected efforts at revitalization succeed, (3) en-

APPENDIX A

courage and recognize small churches and their pastors when they make a difference, and (4) keep developing resources and programs specifically targeted for the denomination's own distinctives.

Mentor Promising Younger Pastors

In the survey results describing the most helpful mentors it was a bit surprising to see how many pastors listed denominational leaders. Although four of the fourteen identified as denominational leaders were affirmed only for their ideas, techniques, and resources, the ten remaining mentors were praised more for their affirming and encouraging roles. These conference and district "executives" or "superintendents" were described using the following accolades: "affirming," "a true friend," "always stressed evangelism and being oneself," "expressed personal concern and deep commitment to the cause of growth," "offered encouragement," "always there to advise and listen to me," "being there to give direction when needed," "really helpful in counseling me in my pastoral work," "he showed me how to work at the basics of preaching, pastoral care, and Christian education" and "had it not been for his support, I probably would have left the ministry."

Serving smaller churches can often be disheartening. Almost all of us who have been there and survived, remember someone who helped us "hang on" when there seemed to be no light at the end of the tunnel. Denominational leaders who are themselves skilled and experienced, and really have a heart for encouraging others, play a very important role in the lives of pastors new to the ministry. But other stories are often told of district executives who seem almost entirely insensitive to this role. Are denominations actually training and encouraging their judicatory leaders to serve in this way, or, for pastors needing a mentor, is it only "the luck of the draw"?

The results obtained from this survey seem to warrant additional attention to mentoring as a priority task for denominational administrators in the field. Under most denominational systems they have influence or even responsibility for determining a pastor's next placement, but their first priority ought to be assisting them where they are now. It is clear from the survey comments

APPENDIX A

that this ministry of encouragement involves more than just a pat on the back. Being available and demonstrating a readiness to listen, offering guidance and suggestions, and manifesting personal commitment to effective ministries in evangelism and church growth are all involved in this denominational calling. Denominational leaders need to function as transformational leaders, not transactional leaders. Perhaps in the training sessions offered for new judicatory leaders this element of serving as mentor deserves a new look and some additional instructional orientation.

Support Special Projects

Some denominations are experimenting with special "Revitalization" programs designed to assist churches bordering on the edge of extinction. One such program was developed by the Church of God, General Conference and is administered by Jim Moss, Church Growth and Evangelism Assistant to the Conference Superintendent. Several Church of God, General Conference congregations have benefited from the intensive conference leadership and funding invested in their revitalization. The story of one of these, York First Church pastored by Gil Livingston, was reported in chapter 7.

The Church of God "Revitalization" program attracted interest even across denominational lines. Mary Jane Myer, pastor of the Jennersville Church of the Brethren in West Grove, Pennsylvania describes her church's experience:

> A year and a half ago, the church decided to move into a revitalization program with the Atlantic Northeast District. We are most grateful for the financial assistance and guidance we are receiving through the District. The heavy organizational structure was dismantled and a Steering Committee of five people was formed. There are two members, the Moderator, and the Pastor from the Jennersville congregation, and a representative from each of our Partner Churches. Mechanic Grove and the Mountville congregations have been an enormous support as we move forward with our vision.

Pastor Myer adds that the grounds and building have been renovated and "transformed into a beautiful and welcoming place." Volunteer "missioners" from the Partner Churches worked at many tasks including extensive efforts to contact and invite the

161

community to the "new" church at the old site. Over the course of two years the average worship attendance almost doubled, Sunday school went from sixteen to twenty-seven, and the phone began to ring as new families called to find out what the church believed and how they might become part of the congregation. Mary Jane Myer closes her "thank you" letter published in the District Newsletter with these words:

> We have a calling and a vision. Thanks to you, the support of our District Executives, Ben and Nancy Wenger and Luke and Anna Brandt, our Missioners, your prayers, and the Holy Spirit, we want to become all that God has in mind for this church in this community. To God be the glory!

Denominations with Partner Church Programs and District Executives skilled in and committed to revitalization, can often make a great difference in the sense of momentum and hope needed for bringing dying churches to new life. Some pastors make it happen on their own. They do all the work to locate and secure the needed financial support and the partnership efforts from other churches. But it is far more helpful for struggling congregations to sense that the "family" hasn't forgotten them, and that their denominational leaders have a plan and the personnel needed to put it in place. When churches are sick and suffering, just as when parishioners are "down," they need to know they are remembered, loved, cared for, prayed for, encouraged, counseled, and visited by Christian brothers and sisters who help them rally, regain strength, and get back on their feet.

Encourage and Recognize Success

Another very helpful role of the denomination is to acknowledge and encourage the efforts of small churches and their pastors. One example of how this ministry of encouragement can be accomplished is found in this story from Georgia. The United Methodist statewide newspaper ran an ad with the following headline: "THE ADVOCATE IS LOOKING FOR 'NEW MINISTRY' IDEAS. Yours may win an 'Advocate Award.' "

The Reverend Robert Vickery had been at his new appointment only a few months when he saw the ad. On the Sunday he arrived to lead his new congregation of forty-seven members, only sixteen actually showed up for worship. But full of hope that God could make a difference, he went to work trying to create a new vision of outreach. One of the church's efforts seemed worthy to report to the Advocate so he responded with a short article telling of their "ministry idea." In fact, the Andersonville United Methodist Church won the first $50 prize and later was awarded the first "Advocate Award." The write-up in the Advocate reads as follows:

> The Advocate Award for the most creative New Ministry this month goes to the Andersonville United Methodist Church in the Americus District. The Rev. Robert L. Vickery is pastor. A $50 check is being sent to the church for this New Ministry.
> With only 57 members, the church has started a weekday program for children which is reaching 47, most of whom have not been attending Sunday School or church services. Arrangements have been for the school bus to stop Tuesday afternoon at the church and let those children off who want to participate in the program. They sing, learn scripture and play; but portions of the time are spent making crafts and gifts which they deliver to shut-ins and persons in the hospitals or someone who needs a special life. They presented a musical at Christmas to a packed house.
> Congratulations Andersonville!

Their own sense of success and empowerment was tremendously enhanced by this recognition and the church has made great strides forward renewed in confidence. What denominational leaders do and say matters—for better and for worse.

Probably many good ideas for how to best recognize and encourage faithful and effective pastors and churches have yet to be discovered. But denominational leaders will do well to keep listening and trying to find ways to repeat for all to hear the words, "Well done, thou good and faithful servant."

Offer Training and Produce Helpful Resources

Although this is a day when large churches, independent experts, interdenominational networks, and even seminary based "centers" are marketing some excellent resources and training opportunities, the pastors in our study indicate that they have benefited also from denominational materials, training events, and programs.

It appears that pastors and congregations in smaller denominations benefit even more from the counsel and programs of their denominational leaders than do those serving in larger denominations. Perhaps they feel more intimately connected to their leaders, or perhaps they have a greater sense of projecting and protecting their unique identity and mission than do those in larger denominations. Whatever the case, it can be said that turnaround pastors utilize the best denominational resources available to them.

An example of this is the large number of pastors in the Church of the Brethren who affirmed the "Passing on the Promise" program. Its basic components are:

1. *Evangelism Leaders Academy*—an annual training experience for clergy and lay teams held in several locations across the nation featuring nationally recognized speakers.
2. *Evangelism Discovery Events*—events designed for congregations to gain fresh perspectives on mission, evangelism and congregational growth.
3. *Friendship Evangelism Emphasis*—an eight-week video training experience aimed at enhancing faith sharing and invitation, and culminating in a Friendship Sunday.
4. *Congregational Self-study and Follow-through*—tools to help a congregation examine itself and the community in order to identify needs and generate action ideas and activities.
5. *Study/Action Units*—resources for four months of study and action focused on four themes: reaching out, inviting, including, and challenging persons to grow in Christian discipleship.
6. *District Support Meetings/Congregational Advisor*—annual district meetings provide for networking ideas and mutual sharing while an outside volunteer congregational advisor offers regular checkups and encouragement.

In a recent conversation with one of the persons creating this program, it was clear that limited financial resources and personnel require them to prioritize their efforts. They select carefully the most important things, produce superior materials, and invest quality support for training and follow-up. Perhaps there is a secret here not only for smaller denominations. Some larger denominations continue to produce excellent resources, but often cut back their field staff in evangelism and church growth to the point that few congregations are exposed adequately to the materials and programs. This leads to an even greater sense of distance between the local church and program agencies, and ultimately fewer local churches making use of the denominational resources.

When Jesus offered the disciples the image of the vine and the branches recorded in John 15, he reminded them that his Father was the vinedresser who pruned the branches that bore some fruit that they might bear even more fruit. Careful pruning can multiply the productivity of a grapevine tenfold. Some of the smaller "branches" of the vine seem to have learned the lesson of pruning earlier than many of the larger branches. It may be time again to reflect on the lessons Jesus intended to teach through this simple but powerful image. It would seem these lessons are equally valid for small or large denominations, and small or large churches.

Joined and Knit Together

When the Apostle Paul expressed his concern for Christ's church to function at its best, he counseled each member to contribute his or her own special gift of ministry with a view toward enhancing the whole. We usually view this "body" imagery as addressed to individual congregations. But today it is fitting that Paul's words are heard at all levels of the body of Christ to help us realize again how critically interdependent we are. Whether pastor or teacher, prophet or evangelist, lay leader or new convert, seminary professor or district superintendent, we are members together of one body "joined and knit together." Let these words then remind us all of how we are to care for and work with one another for the glory of God, the renewal of the church, and the salvation of the world.

> The gifts he gave were that some would be apostles, some prophets, some evangelists, some pastors and teachers, to equip the saints for the work of ministry, for building up the body of Christ, until all of us come to the unity of the faith and of the knowledge of the Son of God, to maturity, to the measure of the full stature of Christ. We must no longer be children, tossed to and fro and blown about by every wind of doctrine, by people's trickery, by their craftiness in

deceitful scheming. But speaking the truth in love, we must grow up in every way into him who is the head, into Christ, from whom the whole body, joined and knit together by every ligament with which it is equipped, as each part is working properly, promotes the body's growth in building itself up in love. (Eph. 4:11-16)

APPENDIX B
List of Participating Pastors and Churches

Key to Denominational Abbreviations
AOG — Assemblies of God
CRC   Christian Reformed Church
COB — Church of the Brethren
COGA — Church of God, Anderson
COGGC — Church of God, General Conference
DOC — Christian Church, Disciples of Christ
PCUSA — Presbyterian Church, USA
UMC — United Methodist Church

Pastor	*Church*
Calvin Aardsma	Knollbrook CRC, Corvallis, OR
Thomas W. Albert	Salem-Berne UMC, Hamburg, PA
Paul Anderson	First COGGC, Harrisburg, PA
Anthony Louis Antonelli	Black Creek UMC, Panama City, FL
David W. Baldridge	Trinity UMC, Plant City, FL
Ray Barkey	Maple Grove COB, New Paris, IN
Stanley Barkdoll	Downsville COB, Kearneysville, WV
Billy J. Bass	Providence UMC, Georgiana, AL
Patty L. Beagle	Independence UMC, Wellsburg, WV
Eric A. D. Bell	Trinity UMC, Rainsville, AL
Timothy R. Boeglin	Bethel UMC, Arlington, TX
David Bromstad	Notasulga UMC, Notasulga, AL

APPENDIX B

Mark Buchanan	Oak Meadow UMC, San Antonio, TX
R. David Chambers	Millington COGGC, Millington, MI
Robert L. Chapman	Arcadia COB, Arcadia, FL
Michael D. Cloyd	Christ UMC, Palm Bay, FL
Bob Coleman	Arnold's Chapel UMC, Bessemer, AL
Creg Crispell	Carlton UMC, Waterport, NY
Larry M. Dentler	North Liberty COB, North Liberty, IN
Joseph F. DiPaolo	Wissinoming UMC, Philadelphia, PA
James Steven Drury	Grassland UMC, Catlettsburg, KY
Ronald Dull	Greenvillage COGGC, Shippensburg, PA
Jeff Dunn	Christ UMC, Bennettsville, SC
Don Duvall	First UMC, Big Lake, TX
Bob Edwards	Judsonia UMC, Little Rock, AR
Kendal Elmore	Pine Creek COB, North Liberty, IN
Eugene L. Feagin	Aldersgate UMC, Inman, SC
Barbara Florey	Concord UMC, Concord, MI
Larry A. Frank	Conestoga UMC, Conestoga, PA
Sylvester Gillespie	Grace UMC, Los Angeles, CA
John Goering	Lewis UMC, Lewis, KS
J. R. Gonzales	Westwood AOG, Westwood, CA
Don Graham	St. Peter's UMC, Corpus Christi, TX
Dennis Hamshire	Green Street COGGC, Harrisburg, PA
J. Val Hastings, Jr.	Emmanuel UMC, Brownstown, PA
William N. Hay, Sr.	Rayman COB, Friedens, PA
Richard Hayward	Linda Vista PCUSA, San Diego, CA
Leonard Higgins	St. Andrew UMC, Fort Smith, AR
Thomas D. Hindman	Penfield UMC, Penfield, PA
John Homer	The Salvation Army, Battle Creek, MI
Dale Hylton	Hatfield COB, Hatfield, PA
Darrin Lee Jones	Salem UMC, Dallas, WV
Donald Jones	Bandana UMC, Bandana, KY
William R. Keeffe	Bow Mills UMC, Bow, NH
Ed Kerr	Plainview UMC, Plainview, AR
Tom Kraft	Pendleton Center UMC, No. Tonawanda, NY
John Kuritz	Farm Hill UMC, Cantonment, FL
Duane A. Lewellen	Newville COB, Newville, PA
Chris Livermore	Torrance UMC, Torrance, PA
Gil Livingston	York First COGGC, York, PA
William Longenecker	Steven's Hill COGGC, Elizabethtown, PA
O. Phillip May	Marvell UMC, Marvell, AR
S. Rene McKenzie	Boca Grande UMC, Boca Grande, FL
Richard D. Moore	Maple Hill UMC, Howard City, MI
Kirk W. Morledge	First PCUSA, Waunakee, WI
Paul C. Murphy	Mt. Gilead UMC, Shermans Dale, PA

APPENDIX B

Mary Jane Myer	Jennersville COB, West Grove, PA
Marcelle G. Myers	Nesby Chapel UMC, Nahunta, GA
Hal Noble	St. Mark UMC, Anniston, AL
Willis E. Osban	Manila UMC, Manila, AR
J. Fred Parklyn	Alice Focht-Memorial UMC, Birdsboro, PA
Gregg Parris	Union Chapel UMC, Muncie, IN
Sharon Patch	St. Mark's UMC, Jacksonville, FL
Richard A. Paul	White City UMC, Fort Pierce, FL
Linda M. Peabody	Vernon UMC, Vernon, CT
Donald E. Peters, Jr.	Nanty-Glo COB, Nanty-Glo, PA
Hazel J. Porter	Good Shepherd UMC, Jacksonville, FL
Steven J. Porter	First UMC, Ringgold, LA
Linda Poteete-Marshall	Trinity UMC, Whittier, CA
W. Ford Price	Humphreys Memorial UMC, Tornado, WV
Yolanda Pupo-Ortiz	Bethesda Hispanic UMC, Bethesda, MD
L. V. Rigney	Pathway COGGC, Blytheville, AR
C. Martin Riley	Miakka UMC, Sarasota, FL
Dennis O. Rinehart	Otterbein UMC, Warren, OH
Eduardo Roque	Monte Olivar UMC, Utuado, PR
Edward Rosenberry	Plainfield First COGGC, Plainfield, PA
R. Branson Sheets III	Pleasant Grove UMC, Bailey, NC
Gerald Shoap	Hanover First COGGC, Hanover, PA
Richard Shover	Camp Hill COGGC, Camp Hill, PA
Ruth Lantz Simmons	Edgelawn UMC, Parkersburg, WV
Bryan E. Siverly	Waverly UMC, Waverly, IL
Patricia A. Small	Alexander Memorial UMC, Jacksonville, FL
Billy D. Strayhorn	First UMC, Groesbeck, TX
Jim Sullivan	The Salvation Army, Las Vagas, NV
Lowell H. Swisher	Wesley UMC, Alamogordo, NM
Wee-Li Tan	Church of All Nations UMC, Boston, MA
James Thomas	Bevertown COGGC, Todd, PA
Richard F. Thornton	Yocumtown COGGC, Etters, PA
James A. Vander Slik	Sunlight Community CRC, Port St. Lucie, FL
Tom Vencuss	Pleasant Valley UMC, Pleasant Valley, NY
Bob Vickery	Andersonville UMC, Andersonville, GA
J. Peter Vosteen	Cloverdale CRC, Boise, ID
Grace C. Washington	Flat Shoals UMC, Decatur, GA
Duane W. Waters	Harbour Heights UMC, Port Charlotte, FL
Earl F. Watterson	Fairview UMC, Petrolia, PA
Roger P. Windell	The Salvation Army, Grand Forks, ND
Norma Wingo	Bethesda UMC, Durham, NC
Charles & Linda Yarborough	First Christian DOC, Albany, KY
Richard Zamostny	Parkwood UMC, Edgewater, MD
Maximilian Zurdt	Stone Glen COGGC, Dauphin, PA